BESTSELLING FICTION BY KRISTEN MARTIN

Shadow Crown

The Alpha Drive
The Order of Omega
Restitution

be your own

#GOALS

YOUR GUIDE TO LIVING YOUR TRUTH, RECLAIMING YOUR SELF-WORTH, AND LOVING YOURSELF EVERY STEP OF THE WAY

KRISTEN MARTIN

BLACK FALCON PRESS

Be Your Own #Goals

Copyright © 2018 by Kristen Martin

Black Falcon Press, LLC

P.O. Box 1879

Montgomery, TX 77356

http://www.blackfalconpress.com

ISBN: 978-0-9979092-5-8 (paperback)

First paperback edition: May 2018

10 9 8 7 6 5 4 3 2 1

For my girlboss fam, my soultribe —
together we will move mountains.

contents

be your own #GOALS

Foreword

BY KAILA WALKER

I THINK EVERYONE has a greater level of consciousness telling them they have the ability to create something more than they are currently leading the world to believe. Even if that passion or road map isn't highlighted with neon signs, the curiosity pulls you enough to let you know there is something more. Something that needs to be pursued. Something that keeps you up at night, wondering.

Sometimes in life, we are lucky enough to be pulled toward some type of teacher to lead with the guidance and courage to support us in knowing we are worth more. For tens of thousands of people Kristen is an online mentor providing invaluable tips on how she became an Amazon bestselling author and designed a life she loves.

She was someone I looked up to online before meeting her had even crossed my mind. But when we met in person, I gained an entirely new level of respect for her—particularly when we stayed up way too late, talking about everything and anything. We laughed in between our talks about struggles, and I discovered how Kristen constantly reframed her state of mind and strived for more.

That night, I learned that sometimes the Universe has a way of guiding you to the right people, and the right situations, even if it's not in your ideal time frame. Sometimes I wonder how I got so lucky to finally be pushed in the direction of Kristen, but I like to believe each person comes into your life to teach you a lesson that needed to be learned and to shine a light on something that may have been dimmed.

If there is one key takeaway I've learned from masterminding with her, it is to act like the woman you know you truly are even if you don't feel like it. Surround yourself with women of the caliber you know you are meant to be surrounded by, and don't be afraid to empower everyone around you as if you were already where you wanted to be. Embody the woman you see yourself becoming in five years so you are always stretching yourself to be more. The hardest part of this lesson to grasp was that sometimes you have to go faster than you're comfortable with so you don't have time to look back and doubt yourself.

As you continue to rise to become the woman of your dreams, protect your energy and hold space for creation and those who add value. Those toxic people you are holding onto—the ones who aren't adding value—may be taking up the time of someone who can take you further. You will start attracting the right people into your life by letting the Universe know what standard you've set for your highest self.

We all want to leave an impact on the world, and kindness and knowledge ripple into something much greater and imprint a higher vibration onto the Universe. I can only imagine how the world would look if we all let down our fears and started sharing our message like the vulnerability in this book.

Although her videos give insights that are invaluable when it comes to leveling up, this book is really a transparent look at Kristen's life. The quality of her reality is shaped by her mindset, giving her the ability to consistently get past the points of self-doubt people tend to give up at.

This book breaks down your belief systems and really has you question the identity you've created for yourself. It may even challenge the excuses you've fabricated in your mind that may have been holding you back. Start visualizing and manifesting a reality you're in love with because you already are that woman of your dreams—you just have to act like it.

I am so excited for your journey and the impact this book will have on you because I know how much Kristen has changed my life. I am lucky enough to call her one of my best friends, and by the end of this book, you will see why.

♡ Kaila Walker

"Surround yourself with people who remind you more of your future than your past." - Dan Sullivan

chapter one

YOU COME FIRST, ALWAYS

"YOU HAVE PRE-cancerous cells in your body."

Not exactly the words I wanted, nor expected, to hear from my doctor at 27 years young. I'm (what I would call) a healthy gal. I've always been physically active, playing *all* the sports in high school, and I've done my best to "eat clean" and take care of myself. I've even reframed my way of thinking about food as "fuel"—give your body the good stuff, and it'll run like a well-oiled machine; bog it down with processed foods and trans fats, and it'll burst at the seams. So to hear the phrase "pre-cancerous cells" leave my doctor's mouth was not only shocking; it felt, at the time, implausible.

As I left the doctor's office in a haze, I remember somehow holding myself together at the front desk, *and* down the elevator, *and* out the double sliding glass doors—I even made it to my car without crying.

But once I slammed that driver's side door shut, it ALL hit me. Tears streamed down my face, my heart fell into my stomach, and my sobbing grew louder and more uncontrolled. I remember looking down at my body, cursing it, wondering why this was happening to me.

What had I done to deserve this?

If there's one thing I hate more than anything, it's throwing myself a pity party. But in that moment, in the confines of my car, it's all I could do to keep from losing it entirely—although a large part of me felt as though I already had.

As gut wrenching and earth-shattering as that day was, it was also the day where something in me *shifted*—something *big*. It dawned on me that I felt, and had felt for many years, undeniably unfulfilled—that I was merely an audience member watching my one precious life flash before my very eyes.

The girl who'd wake up, get in the shower, get ready, make herself a cup of coffee, grab a string cheese for breakfast, and rush out the door, yelling at traffic and cursing the humidity. I'd work my eight hours a day, clicking around on my computer, doing whatever corporate things I thought I should be doing until 5 P.M. I'd then leave the office, get in my car, try to persuade myself that I should cook something healthy, but ultimately choose a drive-thru meal anyway, get home and pour myself a glass (or two or three) of wine and drown my reality in show after show on Netflix. Sound familiar?

It was my full-scale version of hell. It was mind numbing. And I was completely and absolutely *miserable*. I woke up each day knowing exactly what the day would hold—get ready, work, eat, sleep, repeat.

As a typical Type-A humanoid would, I had gone to a good college, maintained over a 3.0 GPA, graduated on time, and then went on to say *sayonara* to my waitressing job—where I served barbecue ribs and giant heaps of mashed potatoes on the daily to overly health-conscious people—to apply for jobs that would (fingers crossed) jumpstart my career. This is what I *thought* I was supposed to be doing. Get a good degree, get a good job so I didn't have to waitress for the rest of my life and could be financially stable on my own, and then work . . . like a freaking robot drone for the rest of my life?

Is that all there is?

Really?

I knew there had to be more.

As fate would have it, in 2014—a year before this whole "pre-cancer" debacle—I had actually rediscovered my passion for writing. Ha-lle-freakin-lu-jah!

I remember that day so clearly. It was a Saturday afternoon and I had just finished watching the *Matrix* movies (I'd also just finished reading a young adult dystopian novel, so it's safe to say my brain was experiencing creative overload). I'd gotten up from the couch after watching the last *Matrix* movie and wandered into my bedroom that, at the time, doubled as my office.

I pulled open the lower desk drawer and rifled through old folders and notebooks, until finally landing on the manila folder I'd been looking for. I took a deep breath as I opened it. My *unfinished* new adult contemporary manuscript sat before me. I spent the day reading it, combing through what I had written. When I'd finished reading it, I'd almost felt like crying. It was terrible—*atrocious*, actually—and the storyline sucked.

Now, I'm not one to speak poorly to myself or think self-deprecating thoughts. But I AM my own harshest critic, and let me tell you, I was **not** happy with what I had written. And so, I left the manuscript on my desk and went back to the couch to Netflix-and-chill all over again.

Rinse. Dry. Repeat.

The next morning—after some much-needed shut-eye after my disastrous reunion with my horrid manuscript— I felt a little better. I went for a run, did some strength training exercises, and made myself a healthy breakfast. I hopped in the shower and I remember while I was shampooing my hair, my thoughts were completely consumed with the concept of alternate realities and dystopian worlds—not surprising after marathon-ing a bunch of science fiction stuff. At this moment in time, I can't recall *exactly* what the thoughts were, but I *can* tell you that my mind was spiralling down the rabbit hole, and fast.

Once I was out of the shower and started to blow dry and straighten my hair, I'll never forget the feeling that came over me. My feet started to tingle and I could hear a pounding in my eardrums as my heart picked up pace. My breath grew shallow and it felt as though a lightning bolt of inspiration had just struck me.

I dropped my straightener on the countertop and staggered backward as idea after idea for a new-and-improved manuscript flooded through my mind. I rushed out of the bathroom—my poor towel hanging onto my skin for dear life—and sat down at my desk, pulling out pens and any other piece of paper I could find.

Sadly, there was no time to fire up my laptop because, admittedly, I can type *much* faster than I can write. But it didn't matter because I spent the next twenty minutes doodling and drawing and writing down all my ideas, how they were all connected, and how my new story could take shape.

After those twenty minutes, I sat back in my desk chair and exhaled a huge sigh of relief. God willing, I fired up my laptop, opened up my manuscript, and that's how my debut novel, *The Alpha Drive*, was born. After rewriting, rewriting again, and self-editing the crap out of this novel, I queried some literary agents to no avail. Nineteen back-to-back rejections. Ouch.

But as Yoda would say, "The force is strong with this one." Those who know me are *hyper*-aware of the fact that I do not take no for an answer, so after doing a ridiculous amount of research, I decided that I was going to take the plunge and self-publish my book. I tentatively set my release date for February 2016.

Well, as you now know, I was thrown for a loop when I found out about my body sabotaging my plans in August 2015, and my surgery was scheduled for October of that same year. After confirming my appointment for surgery, it was then I was slapped in the face with the most crystal-clear realization of all:

That all I *really* wanted to do before I left this Earth was to hold my words — my *book*— in my own two hands.

More specifically, I wanted to see my book, in all its glory—the many pages of paper bound together—and hold a physical copy of **my** book in **my** hands before being gurney-ed into that operating room.

I thought I had worked tirelessly before, but nothing will ever compare to those two months leading up to my surgery. I stayed up until 2 A.M. Some days, I forgot to eat. Most mornings, I woke up in a pile of my own drool on my desk. I was **hell-bent** on making this happen, and I did everything in my power—including paying $60 in expedited shipping—to get my physical paperback book delivered to my doorstep just days before my surgery date. And you know what?

It arrived.

I un-boxed and held *my* book—the book that *I wrote*—in my own two hands for the very first time.

And it wasn't the last time, because to date, I've had the privilege of holding not one, but **four,** of my own books in my own two hands, all of which have become international Amazon bestsellers. And I can honestly say that each time brings with it a feeling of gratitude, aching, and longing. Because I remember that girl—

That miserable, passionless, going-through-the-motions worker-bee ...

That girl who lived for the weekends and dreaded whenever Monday rolled around. That girl who'd had the individuality beaten out of her by society, who told her that she had to be a certain way and do certain things in order to be loved, accepted, and successful. That girl who **knew,** deep down, that there was a way out of her mediocre existence, but couldn't muster up the courage or the strength to even *try*.

It pains me that it took life-threatening news—literally, for the remainder of my life to physically *be in jeopardy*—to finally **shake myself awake** and go after what I'd always wanted, ever since I was a little girl:

To write books. To publish them. To share my message and my voice with the world. To inspire and motivate others to live their best lives and pursue their dreams, no matter how far-fetched they may seem. **To create meaningful content that impacts people on a daily basis**.

This is my mission. This is my purpose. This is my calling.

There is not a single day I wake up and take this life I've built from the ground-up for granted. And whenever I'm having a particularly hard day, I think back to the girl hooked up to the IVs in the hospital—clutching her only copy of her book like it was her *lifeline*—because it was.

That book saved my life.

And *that book* showed me a glimpse of what it felt like . . . to be irrevocably *happy*.

Why start off this book with such a hits-ya-right-in-the-feels kind of story? Because every single one of us on this planet has something in common.

We want to live a happy life.

We also tend to **not** put ourselves first, when we **should** be prioritizing ourselves above everything else, happiness and health included.

I want to debunk a myth right here, right now. Prioritizing yourself doesn't mean you're being self-centered, egotistical, or narcissistic. It's about realizing that what you want and desire is important—it's your Holy Grail and you need to go after it. That aching in your bones, that feeling of wanting more for your life—that desperate need to find and fulfill your purpose, to leave your mark on this world and ultimately leave it better than the way you found it—THAT'S what a happy life is all about.

Another myth I want to debunk is the idea that we "**need**" someone in order to feel "**complete**"—which essentially means that you are not *enough* on your own, as is, and that you'll never live a happy life by yourself. As much as I loved (and still love) the Disney movies and soap operas and romantic comedies where the girl falls in love with the "right" guy and lives happily every after, it's so important to remember that these movies are just that—movies. They are not real. And they certainly don't accurately depict *real life*. Things don't just happen easily and effortlessly, whether we're talking about a relationship, a friendship, going to school, starting a career, etc. There are a *ton* of bumps and hurdles along the way. And yes, the movies may give way and reference these things because every story needs conflict—but I find it to be a sort of *glorified* conflict, one that makes you think, "Hmm, if this terrible thing happens to me, it's okay because Julia Roberts dealt with the same thing and look how her life turned out!"

Just re-read that last sentence and tell me how ridiculous it sounds. We are *comparing* our real life situations with that of a *fictional* storyline. And a lot of the time, that fictional storyline has to do with a guy treating a girl poorly, but ultimately making it up to her, and she forgives him (because that's what a good-hearted girl does, right?) and they stay together and live their life where that same treatment or behavior will likely ensue— but we don't see that part. We only see the beginning, the "honeymoon" phase—not the thirty miserable, heart-wrenching years that follow.

What we don't realize, as women, is that these fictional storylines not only dictate our romantic relationships, they also dictate our family relationships, friendships, interactions with co-workers and bosses—basically our whole social life! We've been conditioned to believe that we need to put *other* people first, even if they're treating us poorly, even if they're making us unhappy, and to forgive all the wrongdoings and continue on with that dismal existence.

Well, I'm here to say SCREW THAT. Screw it right into the cork I'm pushing back into this bottle of wine.

YOU come first. ALWAYS.

Period. The End.

There's a quote I love by Lady Gaga that says, "If you're wondering which way to go, remember that your career will never wake up and tell you that it doesn't love you anymore." Except I like to interchange the word *career* with *passion*. Because, if we're being real here, it's very possible that you could wake up one morning and get fired from your job. Totally plausible.

Your passion, on the other hand, well . . . that's *all* you. That's *your* thing. When it comes to your passion, you have complete control over it with regard to what you do and don't do, what you want and don't want, and whom you want to have involved, if anyone.

The point I'm trying to make is that I made a decision, three years ago, on that hospital gurney, to **put myself first**. I *choose* myself every single day. And I put myself— my wants, dreams, and desires—first because I've discovered the one thing we're lied to about as from a very young age: that you need external **approval** in order to feel loved, accepted, and happy, when really . . .

YOUR happiness is up to YOU.

Seriously. How many times have you caught yourself saying, "When I have this type of lifestyle, and this type of partner, and this type of *whatever*, then and only then will I be happy"?

I'm not gonna lie, I've done it. Guilty as charged.

But only when I came to terms with and wholly accepted that *I* have *complete control* over my own happiness did I understand how damaging this belief could be. It's probably why I've jumped from relationship to relationship and never fully allowed myself to be single—to be alone—and discover who I actually am at my core, and what I truly want in life. It's probably why I've put so much stock into *caring* about what other people think of me, my life path, what I'm doing, and what I'm *not* doing. It's probably why I've felt like I was living someone else's version of happiness—someone else's narrative—**and not my own.**

It takes a lot of courage to buck up and reflect on all of these harsh truths that I just mentioned. It's taken me months of meditation, journaling, reflection, and digging *real* deep to pull out these shortcomings about myself that I haven't wanted to stare in the eye. The paragraph you just read wasn't an easy one for me to write, because I like to think of myself as being really independent, having my shit together, and doing *all* the girlboss things.

But those shortcomings I just mentioned—those unnecessary, yet essential-to-my-growth flaws—certainly don't make me *feel* like a girlboss, nor do they portray me in that way. That's why we have to accept our imperfections and forgive ourselves for past mistakes (which we'll talk more about in the next chapter), because if we don't, we'll *never* move forward. We'll continue to live a half-assed life, just going through the motions each and every day. Please don't live a half-assed life—live a whole-ass one. I beg of you.

So here's the real kicker, and a question that'll probably make you squirm and have you packing and running for the hills . . .

Do you feel like you're living **someone else's version** of happiness and *not your own?*

If you answered yes, don't feel disheartened or ashamed. I want you to know that **you are not alone**. I was doing the exact same thing up until about three years ago, and we'll talk all about that in the coming chapters.

If there's one thing I want you to take away from this chapter, it's this:

YOU are important.

Your HAPPINESS is important.

And YOU are the only person who is going to truly be able to make yourself happy because **true happiness** comes from within.

As of three years ago, there are three major principles I live my life by, and I want to share them with you. I may come across as frank, but I may also be the only person you come across in this one precious life who's ever going to say what needs to be said (and heard), so here goes:

1. **Your sole existence should not be for anyone else except yourself.**

I may get some hate for this one, but hear me out. As painful as it may be to think about, there is always a chance you or your partner could suddenly have a change of heart and decide to go your separate ways. Per the American Psychological Association's study in 2017, about 40% to 50% of married couples in the United States divorce. Just like there's no stopping your kids from growing up and becoming adults who will then go on to procreate and form their own families, there's also no denying that eventually, we all age to the point where we move onto the next realm and are no longer on this Earth. I know it sounds morbid, and you're absolutely right—it is. But only by focusing on this bigger picture will you understand just how important it is to *do the things you want to do when you want to do them.* Stop living for other people and start living *for yourself.*

2. **Material things may make you happy in the short-term, but long-term happiness must come from within.** The harsh reality about acquiring material things is that they only make you feel happy *for a time.* They are temporary and fleeting. Eventually, you'll want to move out of that house you worked so hard to buy in order to move into a bigger house; or your car—the one that used to be your dream car—will feel outdated and you'll want the newest model. Essentially, what ends up happening is that you'll suddenly feel that something "isn't good enough" any longer, and you'll look for the next newest thing. Don't get me wrong—it's okay to want nice things and it's okay to have goals to acquire these things. Just don't fall into

the "I'll be happy when . . ." trap. YOU are worth more than those material things. Think of if this way: you can put a price tag on material items, but you cannot put a price tag on your happiness.

3. **Everything you've ever wanted is on the other side of fear.** Is going after what your core desires scary? Absolutely! Can reaching success feel impossible at times? More often than you might think. But is it worth it? Oh yes. 1,000 times YES. Right now, your dreams, passions, and desires may seem really far-fetched. *How do I even get started? Where I am going to find the time? Where I am going to get the money to pay for it all?* When you focus on all the what-ifs and all the things you *don't* have, it's really not all that surprising when you eventually find yourself backed into a corner, paralyzed by fear. I will admit, starting is the hardest part—it's also the most frightening part. But by breaking your dreams down into smaller, actionable steps, the whole process will become less daunting—and that's exactly what we're going to do right now. So go grab a journal or a notebook and answer the questions in the following exercises. Each chapter will end like this because in order to be your own **#goals**, you have to take the time and do the work to discover what **#goals** actually looks like *for you*, no one else.

BYOG ACTION 1: Write down every single thing that makes you happy, no matter how big or small—singing at the top of your lungs in the shower, drinking your favorite coffee in the morning, reading a super cheesy romance novel, going to a nightclub and dancing with your girlfriends, cuddles on the couch by a fire with your significant other, kids, or furbabies—write them all down. Skip a line or two underneath each thing you write—it'll make action 2 easier.

BYOG ACTION 2: On the same list, in the margins, rate each item on a scale of 1 to 5 (five being most often and one being least often). You can use the numbers more than once because I'm sure you have more than five things on your list.

BYOG ACTION 3: Now look at the list with your ratings and circle the top 3-5 activities that make you feel the most excited or that, in a "perfect world", you wish you could do every single day.

BYOG ACTION 4: Take a second to reflect on what number you wrote next to those particular activities. I'm guessing they're probably in the lower end of the spectrum, on the 1-3 scale. Think about this for a minute. These are the things that make you **most excited,** but are the things you do the **least often**. Let the irony of that sink in.

BYOG ACTION 5: In the space below these 3-5 items, write down the main thing that is holding you back from doing them more often. These could be things like money, time, fear of starting, fear of failing, fear of judgment, etc. You'll have to go deep here, so be as open and honest as possible.

BYOG ACTION 6: For those same 3-5 items, write down one action step you can take *this week* to move one step closer toward doing that activity more regularly. Perhaps one of the things you listed was international travel and the limiting factor is that you don't have enough money. Your action step might be that you open up a savings account and deposit $75 by the end of this week. If you continue to deposit $75 by the end of every week for 4 months ($75 * 4 weeks = $300/month), then you will have saved up a decent chunk of money, $1,200, ($300 * 4 months = $1,200), which can easily buy you a plane ticket for international travel. If you don't want to wait 4 months to travel, you'll have to deposit more money each week, but I'm sure you get the idea here.

Starting is the hardest part, but by completing one small action each week, you'll bring yourself one step closer to doing the things you love to do—and doing them more often. If *time* happens to be your major limiting factor, don't fret, because we'll discuss time management in greater detail in chapter five. Once we recognize and face what we think is limiting us, then, and only then, can we can put a plan in place to overcome it.

Closing Thought :

"If not now, when? If not you, who?"

–Hillel The Elder

chapter two

ACCEPT YOUR FLAWS

OH LORDY, IF I tried to count the number of mistakes I've made in my life, I would run out of numbers. Not even kidding.

For the sake of total transparency, I'm writing this particular chapter in the evening after a long day at work, and I've already had two glasses of red wine—an oaky Cabernet, for those who might be curious. I'm telling you this because I want you to know that this was *intentional*— if we're going to be talking about flaws, (and if I'm going to be divulging *my own* flaws), what can a little liquid courage hurt? Nothing. It's actually completely necessary in order to get through the pain and embarrassment of revealing them right here, right now.

I digress. So yes, flaws. We all have them. It's part of being human. There are some of us who shy away from our flaws, pretend they don't exist, and only focus on our positive attributes. There are some of us who focus *only* on our flaws and constantly doubt ourselves and play it safe our whole lives for fear of those flaws being exposed. But then, there are those rare few who look at their flaws and *accept* them for what they are, and only attempt to change them for the better—whether that's for their own benefit, for the greater good, or, in many cases, both.

I so wished I fell into this latter category, but unfortunately, I fall into the first one. I rarely self-doubt, nor do I self-loathe, and I rarely experience imposter syndrome (which is when you can't appreciate your accomplishments for what they are and build it up in your head that you're actually a fraud who will eventually be exposed). I am perfectly aware of what my shortcomings are, but a lot of the time, I simply just ignore them and keep doing my thing.

But wait . . . isn't this chapter about *accepting* your flaws? And by ignoring them and pretending they don't exist, aren't you, in a way, *accepting* them?

Not really.

Just because I ignore my flaws doesn't mean I've accepted them. I simply graze over them and focus on the positive. While this can be useful when you're trying to achieve a short-term goal, it certainly isn't the best long-term strategy. It may feed my ego, but in doing so, it starves my heart.

In order to be sincerely happy for the long-term, you need to be able to accept your flaws for what they are. You must learn to **love** your imperfections. And if one day, you decide to improve upon said flaw, then that motivation and drive has to come from an internal yearning. It has to be because *you* want to improve. External reasons won't work—again anything "outward" is only a short-term fix. If there's one thing you'll hear over and over again throughout this book, it's that everything you do, you have to do for you, and the decision-making—the desire—has to come from within.

I'm going to share my three biggest flaws, and I'm also going to share how they've held me back. It took me quite some time to come to these realizations and, let me tell you, they weren't easy pills to swallow. I'm still working on myself, and by no means have I mastered this whole "accepting my flaws" thing, but it's something I work toward each and every day. This is as much a self-discovery process for me as it is for you. Hopefully by reading about my own flaws and what I've learned from them, it'll make it less intimidating to really look inside yourself and admit your own shortcomings.

Let's start with numero uno. My number one flaw, BY FAR, is that I am a **control freak**. When I was younger, I used to make up stories and white lies to maintain control. The example I'm about to share is downright ridiculous, and my cheeks are *burning* with shame at the mere thought of sharing this, but here goes.

When I was in fifth grade, my family moved from Indiana to Arizona in the middle of the school year—which, at the time, was like moving from Farmville to Hollywood. I wasn't exactly the cutest kid in my middle-school-years; I had frizzy hair (I hadn't learned what a straightener was yet), GOLD braces (yes, I had a grill before grills were even a thing—take that, Nelly! Trendsetter right here), round-Harry-Potter-like-glasses (because what 5th grader isn't terrified of sticking a foreign object such as a contact lens in their eye?), and severely bushy eyebrows (in which my parents would always say, "But sweetheart, they give you *character*.")

So yep, at age eleven, I was bullied as a kid. The name-calling, the teasing, the air of inferiority I felt as I walked through the halls in my overalls and oversized sweatshirt—I was lucky enough to experience the whole kit-and-caboodle. I remember suffering through "the new kid" syndrome for a few weeks until something (that should have been miraculous, but obviously wasn't) happened. A *new* "new kid" joined my fifth grade class. Hallelujah! I was saved! All the attention would shift to him!

Not so fast, Nancy.

Turns out, I was the poor unfortunate soul who got the new "new kid" in her class that everyone *loved*. He was the class clown, and my classmates *adored* him. And why wouldn't they? He was hilarious!

But what else do class clowns do besides goof off?

Find weaker prey to feast on.

Hello, my name's Kristen and I HAVE A GRILL.

As I was desperately trying to gain back control of my life and my dignity after the first round of bullying, I found myself the target yet again. I *hated* not feeling in control of my life and how other people were treating me. I hated being misperceived and picked on for no god damn reason.

So I told a white lie.

At the time, Britney Spears had just entered the scene. If the entire female population of my school could have dressed up in scandalous schoolgirl outfits with braids donned with fuzzy-ball hair ties without being called into the principal's office for violating the dress code, we would have had hundreds of tiny Britney-wannabes running around the campus. The outpouring of love for Britney knew no bounds.

And that's when an idea HIT ME (baby one more time)—one that would get my class off my back and hopefully stop the bullying for good.

I told my entire class that I knew Britney Spears.

And to prove it, I even went so far to forge a signature on the insert of the CD (that's compact disc, for all you young folk) and brought it to school to show off. I kept up the façade for a while until eventually the "next big thing" happened and people forgot about Kristen's "amazingly realistic connection" to the biggest pop star of that time.

I suppose I've always been a natural born storyteller.

So, did it work? Surprisingly, yes. My classmates started treating me with respect because they didn't want me to "put in a bad word with Britney" (reading this back, I'm cracking up because it's just sooo ridiculous, but it's the truth). This certainly ties into wanting to be accepted, but for me, I wanted so desperately to take back control of my feelings and my perceived "coolness" that I was willing to make up a preposterous story and stick with it. In my mind, I figured if I could *control* the story, then I could *control* the way I was perceived. It worked, but moral here is that it didn't feel good. So I saved my white lies and storytelling for my notebooks, where I could let my imagination run wild and make up all the nonsense my little heart desired.

Unfortunately, my sense of control carried on into my later years, although it took different forms. In my romantic relationships, when things wouldn't go my way and I felt myself losing control, I'd behave in such a way to try and *control* the other person. This included giving ultimatums, playing the "Well-what-if-this-happens" game, and other shenanigans I'm certainly not proud of. In college, I developed an eating disorder in order to "control" my appearance. I'd eat very little, then binge-drink, then binge-eat, then throw it up the next morning. Definitely not proud of that one. In my corporate career, I'd attempt to take control of *every* important project and work myself to death in the hopes that I would prove that I deserved the coveted promotion. And even now, in my author journey, I see control creep in. I honestly think it's why I chose to self-publish. I don't want anyone to tell me that "because my book isn't selling, it's going to be pulled from the shelves" or that "as the author, you have zero say in the cover design" or that "this entire section needs to be cut and rewritten to make it more commercial".

So yep. I am a control freak to the nth degree.

And it's because I absolutely *hate* uncertainty. Uncertainty gives me anxiety. Anxiety makes me feel out of control. And when I feel out of control, I feel like everything in my life is going to fall apart and implode. This is a **horrifying** feeling, especially when you've worked *so freaking hard* for everything you have. Every now and again, I have to take a step back and remind myself that the things I own are *just things* and that what really matters are my relationships and friendships—two things I need to let flow. I can't control other people, so why bother? You're going to do what you're going to do, and I'm going to do what I'm going to do. Plain and simple. No need for control there.

The memories I create and the legacy I leave behind are also important—again, I can set my intentions for my memories and the legacy I want to leave, but I can't fully control either of these things because I have no power over how other people choose to perceive those same memories or how they choose to perceive my work, my message, and eventually, my legacy. That power lies with them, not me. So again, no need for control here.

Let's move onto my second biggest flaw: I am **incredibly stubborn**.

Fellow Taureans, where you at?!

I'll just say it. I like to have things my way. I like to make my own decisions. I like when people agree with me and support me.

Is it so much to ask that everyone just see my point of view?!

All joking aside, the biggest hindrance when it comes to being so stubborn is that I'm not always receptive to incredible opportunities that are literally staring me right in the face. I mean, they're *right there*. My grabby little control hands could reach out and snatch them right up if they wanted to.

What I've come to learn is that just because something doesn't go my way doesn't mean it'll end up being a dreadful, entirely loathsome experience—it just means it'll be *different* than my expectations—and yet, the former is what I've conditioned myself to think.

The one and only stubborn-of-all-stubborn experiences that immediately comes to mind is when I went on a cruise to Mexico. One of the excursions I'd opted for was driving a beach buggy down the open road to a resort. I was *so excited* to drive this thing because the pictures were irresistibly charming, not to mention I'd be able to post swoonworthy Instagram stories of my pastel pink beach buggy against the backdrop of the cerulean ocean.

It was every photographer-adventurer's dream.

The day of the excursion, I bounded down the ship's steps and flew across the boardwalk, scanning the sea of people for my assigned number. With my nerves buzzing and a smile plastered on my face, I presented my driver's license and was then led, in all its pastel pink glory, to my dream buggy. As I hopped into the driver's seat and revved the engine, my heart sank.

The buggy was a stick shift.

My dad, bless his heart, had tried to teach me how to drive stick when I had turned 16 years old, but at the time, I hadn't seen any practical use for it. I figured we'd have flying cars by the time I was 40, so why bother learning stick? Not to mention, I was *awful* at it.

Hmm, stubborn much?

My vision driving down the highway in my cute pink buggy with the wind whipping through my hair and the sun shining on my face quickly dissipated. My mood immediately turned sour. I told the instructor that I couldn't drive stick and, therefore, couldn't go. He told me I could still go, but that I'd have to sit in the back while someone else drove. Again, being stubborn, I was incredibly reluctant to do this because I'd had this picture in my head and wanted it to go *my way*—I wanted to drive, dammit!—but eventually I caved because I still wanted the experience. And you know what?

I still went down the highway with the wind whipping through my hair and the sun shining on my face. In hindsight, I enjoyed being a passenger *more* than driving because I was able to sightsee and experience everything Mexico had to offer because I didn't have to pay attention to traffic, worry about getting stuck in second gear, or try to keep myself from careening off the edge of the highway into the deep blue and beyond. The only differences to my original vision were: 1) that I wasn't driving, and 2) that I was in a different color buggy. But the *feelings* would have been the same in either situation— wind in hair, sun on face—and that's all that really matters.

From this, I learned that saying yes more often (more on this in chapter eight) opens you up to more opportunities that may, on the surface, appear less-than-ideal, but may end up being the same, if not better, than what you previously imagined.

Tally-ho! Onto my third biggest flaw: I am **overly impatient.** When I decide I want something, I will do *anything* and *everything* I can to get it as fast as I possibly can. Surprisingly, I'm not impatient with my writing projects (this one that you're reading right now has taken me over two years to write), but when it comes to "next steps", I tend to put almost unrealistic, insanely pressure-filled deadlines on myself.

I think back to when I first moved to Texas (only **seven** years ago at the time of writing this), and it feels like a *lifetime* ago. When I think back to high school, I feel like a completely different person inhabited my body. And my childhood? Well, that's a complete and utter blur.

I'm not one to stay still for long. In fact, I'm not sure I actually know how to *be still*. Which means, since I'm always looking ahead to the next thing, I'm never truly present in the moment. I don't take the time to appreciate my current situation, all the things I have, and the many accomplishments I've added to my belt. I don't take the time to revel in each moment and truly appreciate them for what they're worth. Eventually, those moments in time pass, and I'm left wondering why I feel so burnt out.

Learning to be patient is still something I struggle with on a daily basis, but when I sense myself getting anxious or antsy, or starting to set unrealistic deadlines, I remind myself not to get too attached to the outcome and just let things happen as they are supposed to. Everything that is *meant* for you **will** happen for you exactly when and how it's supposed to.

Okay, admitting my flaws wasn't as hard as I thought it would be, thanks—in large part—to my handy dandy glass (or two or three) of wine. And, if you are of the legal drinking age, I'd recommend grabbing a glass of vino (or your choice of adult beverage) before starting on the next exercise.

In order to be able to accept your flaws, you have to get down, dirty, and real with yourself and admit what those imperfections actually are. In all honesty, before drinking some wine, I actually couldn't pinpoint my top three flaws because of my tendency to just brush over them in my daily life. When you ignore something for so long, it eventually goes away, right? (Kidding! That is certainly *not* a good life motto to live by.)

The most important thing here is that you are **completely honest** with yourself. This may not be the most enjoyable exercise, but it's an important one to do on your journey to finding happiness and living your truth.

Think of it this way—coming to terms with your flaws means your skin will only grow thicker. If someone else insults you, criticizes you, or points out one a mistake of yours or an imperfection, it won't matter—because you've already accepted yourself, flaws and all! It's like being a step ahead without anyone else knowing.

BYOG ACTION 7: Time for a little role-play. Imagine you're the manager at work. It's the end of the year, and you're about to give an employee evaluation to someone who is *just like you*—they share the same personality traits, same drive, same mannerisms and quirks, same everything. First, write down this person's top three strengths, then write down their top three areas for improvement. By role-playing, we're putting ourselves in a different situation, and allowing those strengths and weaknesses to come to the surface.

BYOG ACTION 8: Now that you have their (technically your) top three strengths, write down *all* the things these strengths have allowed you to do. For instance, if one of your strengths is time management, you can write down all of the activities/goals you've accomplished in a certain timeframe due to this special skill. If you're strength is independence, you can write down all the ways in which depending on yourself, and no one else, has benefitted your life.

BYOG ACTION 9: Now let's look at your top three weaknesses. Write down *all* the things these weaknesses are keeping you from doing. How are they hindering you? How are they holding you back? For example, let's say one of your weaknesses is that you get distracted really easily. This could be hindering you from reaching a certain goal, or finishing a certain project, or could be making you feel lousy in general because you can't seem to focus on one thing for very long. Then read back what you just wrote. How does it make you feel? Are you frustrated that these flaws have kept you from achieving certain things?

BYOG ACTION 10: Sit back in your chair and put your hand over your heart. Take a deep breath and while looking at your list, say, "These flaws are a part of me, but they do not **define** me." Repeat this until you believe it, every morning when you wake up and every evening before you fall asleep. In doing this, you are proclaiming to the universe that you recognize these imperfections, but that they **do not define you** as a person. You accept them, but you also hold the power to change them, if you so choose.

BYOG ACTION 11: Similar to the last chapter's exercise, write down one action step for each of these flaws that you can take this week—but only *if you want to* and are ready for that next step—to help transition it over to a strength. Using the last example of getting distracted easily, your action step could be setting a timer on your phone to work on a task for 20 minutes at a time. Once your 20 minutes is up, allow for a 10-minute break, and then get back to it for another 20 minutes. Setting a schedule for "work time" and "play time" can help you build the discipline required to stay focused for longer intervals of time.

Closing Thought :

Don't strive to be perfect.

Instead, strive to be perfectly imperfect.

chapter three

EVERYTHING IS A CHOICE

WE'RE GOING TO start this chapter off with another favorite quote of mine: "If you don't like where you are, then move. You are not a tree." In my humble opinion, it sums up exactly what we're going to talk about in this chapter, being that *everything* is a *choice*.

A huge choice I made—and one that has definitely changed my life for the better—was starting an online platform, most notably my YouTube channel. At the time, I was working in a corporate setting in the chemical industry and had just moved about an hour north of Houston. I had a lot of doubts when I first started filming videos—first, I wondered if anyone would even watch them, and second, I worried whether or not becoming an "online personality" would have a negative effect on my corporate career. After making my trusty pros and cons list (something I've been doing since my teenage years), I decided that the potential reward completely outweighed the cons. When it came to how it could potentially affect my career, the worst case scenario was that I'd just have find a job in a different industry—one that was more accepting of its employees spreading their creative wings.

When I made that choice to start my YouTube channel, I didn't look back. I mapped out a business plan, stayed consistent with my content, cultivated and nurtured my community, and brainstormed new video topics like there was no tomorrow. I looked at it as an all-or-nothing thing—commit to it fully, or don't do it at all.

As I've already alluded to, creating this online presence was the **best thing** I've ever done for myself. It's allowed me to connect with likeminded readers and writers from all over the world. It's allowed me to sell thousands of books as a self-published author. It's allowed me to create courses that benefit the people I aim to reach. It's provided a space for my voice to be heard.

I could have put this choice on the backburner for fear of the potential consequences. For fear of the unknown. For fear of judgment, and failure. But I didn't. I made the choice to put myself out there, to inspire others, to share my journey. If there's one thing I regret, it's not making this choice sooner.

Even though I didn't know how this journey was going to turn out, or what sort of impact it would have, what I *do* know, without a shadow of a doubt, is if I hadn't made this decision, I'd be kicking myself, wondering, and complaining about the *what-if.*

What if I had made the choice to start my YouTube channel? What would my life look like? Who would I be impacting? Would I have been happier than I am right now?

If you've found yourself complaining more often than usual as of late, it's likely that it's because of the recent choices you've made. Whether you've just been thrown a curveball at work, or your kids are getting on your last nerve, or that project deadline is approaching, but you have x, y, and z to attend to before you can even think of diving back into said project—everything is a *choice.* Maybe that job opportunity you decided to not even interview for would have resulted in less curveballs at work. Maybe hiring a nanny would have resulted in fewer headaches every time Tommy throws a temper-tantrum. Or maybe pursuing that business idea instead of pushing it to the backburner over and over again would have resulted in more freedom of time.

Everything is a choice.

I'm willing to bet that you know someone (heck,

multiple people) who seems to do one thing and one thing only: whine.

Want to know my biggest pet peeve?

People who complain.

Now I'm not saying that I've never complained before—trust me, I have, and more than I care to admit—but I *rarely* complain anymore. And if I do catch my mouth opening to whine about something, I always count back from three, say whatever it is I was about to say in my head, and *then* decide if it's worth saying out loud. Most of the time, it's not.

Shocker.

You see, when we complain, we're essentially giving a certain situation, person, or thing, the power to rule our thoughts, when, in fact, exactly the opposite is true. Everything we do, say, think, feel, and act on is *a choice*.

While we cannot always control what happens to us, what we do have control over is our *reaction* to it.

Is your mother-in-law being a pain in the arse again? Oh, Martha, why must you make life so difficult? You *could* tell her off and ruin a perfectly good day (and every other event you two plan to attend together in the future), *or* you could make your husband deal with her (it's his mother anyway!), *or* you could choose to be cordial, not let her bother you, and move right along with your day.

Your choice.

Did your demanding boss just hand you yet another

pointless project with yet another impossible deadline? Super! You *could* blow up at them and flip 'em the bird, *or* you could have an adult conversation and ask for an extension on the deadline, *or* you could finally quit and find/create a job you actually enjoy.

Your choice.

Did your significant other just leave their dirty clothes lying around the bathroom floor (yet again) after you've repeatedly asked them to walk the five extra steps to throw them in the hamper? Hunky dory! You could lose your temper and yell at them and bring up the 18 other things that are bothering you (that probably don't have anything to do with this situation) and make the fight even worse, blowing it completely out of proportion, *or* you could calmly and gently prompt them to put their clothes in the hamper, and even put a sticky note on the bathroom mirror to serve as a reminder.

Your choice.

Have I ever lost my temper, blown up at someone, or behaved in a way I wasn't proud of? Absolutely. I wouldn't be human if I hadn't. But I'll tell you what I remember most about those times: how my outlandish reactions made me *feel* afterward. Each and every time, I felt horrendous. I didn't feel like myself. Because "real" Kristen doesn't blow up at people—"real" Kristen is understanding and empathetic, and *chooses* to be patient, positive, and helpful whenever possible.

Just as our reactions are completely our choice, so are

the words we speak. Our words can either plant gardens or burn whole forests down. We can choose to plant the seeds by focusing on the positive (grateful and loving thoughts), or we can choose to ignite the fire by focusing on the negative (complaining, criticizing, and gossiping).

The complaint I hear most often is *I'm unhappy*—unhappy with your job, your relationship, your financial situation, your friendships, your workplace—and yet many of us will remain in these *unhappy* situations for years and years, and most of the time, never leave. We allow the situation *to control us* instead of **taking control** of the situation.

Never lose sight of the fact that you *always* hold the cards—whether or not you choose to lay one down and pick another one up is completely up to you.

Let's use being unhappy in your relationship as an example. As I've already mentioned, I *was* engaged to be married. After almost three years of being engaged, I finally broke off the relationship altogether. Why? Because I was unhappy, and had been for the majority of that relationship. Plain and simple.

Was it devastating calling my family and closest friends and telling them the wedding was off? More than you could possibly imagine. Was it humiliating calling all of the vendors I had worked so closely with and telling them I'd no longer need their services? You betcha.

But the way I *chose* to look at it was as a *momentary lapse* of pain and hurt in exchange for a *lifetime* of happiness and fulfillment. In getting out of my own head (which is almost impossible to do when you're on the verge of heartbreak) and trying to look at the bigger picture, I realized I could survive a year of pain, hurt, and embarrassment if it meant having 60+ years of happiness and fulfillment in being true to myself. Was it the hardest thing I've ever had to do? Yes. But do I regret it? No.

If anything, I regret not doing it sooner.

Unhappy with your job? Find a new one. Unhappy with that next job too? Reevaluate and see if starting your own business is actually what you should have done in the first place. **Your choice.**

Unhappy with your financial situation? Stop buying so much *stuff*. Cut up those credit cards and apply for a loan to consolidate all of your debt and significantly lower the interest you're currently paying. **Your choice.**

Is your relationship weighing you down? Try couples counseling. If that doesn't work, and cutting things off cold turkey scares the bejesus out of you, try a trial separation. Sometimes taking a smaller step toward the end destination is easier than taking a giant leap into the unknown. **Your choice.**

Is one of your friendships eating up all of your time and energy to the point where you're pretending like you didn't see that last text that just came through? If someone feels like a toxic influence, it's probably because *they are*. Stop giving in to the drama and gossip and draining conversations, and establish boundaries with this person. *They* don't need to know about these boundaries, but the quicker you stop engaging with them and enabling these behaviors, the faster they'll get the hint and slowly fade out of your life. **Your choice.**

Are these decisions easy? No, of course not. These are *life-changing* decisions. But if the thought of having a certain something removed from your life gives you a sense of peace and calm, chances are you need to do some removing! Any time I start to feel restless, anxious, or irritated, it's usually because there's something in my life that **doesn't fit anymore**.

As we'll talk more about in chapter nine, the only constant is *change*. As human beings, we are constantly changing and evolving into the people we are meant to be. Not everyone or everything that was once along for the ride on your life path is meant to stay with you into the future. It can be painful to kick 'em off the wagon. It can be painful to let go and say goodbye. But if you don't clear some space in your life, you'll be saying a **premature** goodbye to new people, things, and opportunities that *could* have had an instrumental effect on your life path in getting you to where you'll ultimately end up anyway. Don't be your own roadblock!

BYOG ACTION 12: Write down three things in your life that you've complained about recently—things that maybe aren't going your way. If you have five things or ten things, then great (for this exercise, not for life). Write 'em all down.

BYOG ACTION 13: Now next to each one, write down exactly what it is about that particular situation that's bothering you. So if you hate your job, is it the actual job itself that you dislike, or is it dealing with your ill-tempered boss? Is it a lazy coworker? Is it feeling like you work really hard and aren't getting paid enough? **What is truly bothering you?**

BYOG ACTION 14: Now that you've identified exactly what it is about the situation that's bothering you, write down how you'd want it to look instead (i.e. what would need to change in order to make the situation better?) So if you feel like you work really hard and aren't getting paid enough, perhaps working up the courage to ask for a raise would improve the situation.

BYOG ACTION 15: Only *you* will be able to assess which situations you can improve and which situations need to be removed altogether. The most important thing here is to remember that you *always* have a choice. You hold the cards. You can change your situation if you truly want to. And if you feel like you can't, then do a deep-dive and figure out what's holding you back. More likely than not, it's because you're afraid of something. I've stayed in unhealthy relationships for too long because I was afraid of the unknown that would come after it. It was only when I realized that the "unknown" could be whatever I *wanted* it to be that the choice to end things became a whole lot easier. What are you afraid of? Pushing that fear aside, what choices and options are available to you? I promise, you have a lot more available to you than you might think.

Closing Thought:

You have the power to

change your life for the better.

It's all in the choices you make.

chapter four

YOU ARE WHAT YOU THINK

YOUR MIND IS more powerful than you could ever possibly imagine. It stands to reason, then, that your thoughts—the things you tell yourself, the values and morals you hold dear, those little voices in your subconscious telling you to choose one thing over another—have a much larger effect than what we've been led to believe.

I'm sure you've heard the phrase "You are what you eat" at some point in your life. I've always found this saying interesting. Of course I am what I eat—I'm eating it and it's going inside of my body to become a part of me. But as I've grown older, I've come to understand the deeper meaning behind this saying. And I may come off as a total whack-job after I say this, and I could very well be the only one who thinks this way, but to me, "You are what you eat" actually means "You feel what you eat", in the way you would say, "Oh, you're gonna feel that tomorrow," after a brutal workout or a night of heavy drinking.

It's no secret that eating natural, healthy foods that actually grow from the ground (not ones that go through a chemical processing plant) are healthier for you than highly processed foods. It's also no secret that we tend to feel better when we eat healthier foods. I always know that my body is going to operate better if I opt for a salad versus a steak because the salad contains naturally occurring macro and micro nutrients that my body craves and needs to survive in order to perform at its best.

So yes, *you are what you eat* because if you eat highly processed, sugary, fatty foods all the time, then you're going to feel run-down, lethargic, tired, and lazy. Your body has to work overtime to process and digest these unnatural "foods" you've put into it. But when you eat healthy and nutritious leafy greens, vegetables, and fruits, your body can do its thing and break down the food with a lot less effort because it's *natural.*

I like to think of our minds in the same way. When we

feed ourselves negative, self-limiting, fearful thoughts, our minds are working overtime to process all of these *what-if* scenarios of doubt and worry that haven't even happened yet. Those thoughts end up getting so complex to the point where our minds end up taking detours down Doubt Avenue and Worry Lane. Doubt and worry are just cousins of fear—they have the same effect as fear-based thoughts do, which usually directs us down a road of living a life full of caution and security. Sure, being cautious *sometimes* is okay, and feeling secure isn't all that bad, but to live your *whole* life in fear of experiencing new things because it's *safer* and more *comfortable*? No thank you.

On the flip side, when we feed ourselves positive, uplifting, affirming thoughts, our minds can work as they naturally would (and should) to process these thoughts smoothly, without interruption. This is because positivity is our natural state. And to the many people who may disagree with this, I'd like to point to the only exhibit we need—**Exhibit A: Children**.

Before we grow up to be adults, before we get fired from our first job, before we don't get into the college we wanted, before we experience our first heartbreak, *before the world hardens us*—we are pure and positive and full of light. As children, everything is beautiful and full of wonder. As children, we ask questions and put ourselves out there and take risks climbing the tree because we want to catch the butterfly and have no fear of what might happen if we fall. Falling doesn't even come into the equation.

I'm going to repeat that. Children have no fear of what might happen **if** they are to fall because falling **doesn't even enter the equation**.

As a kid, I imagined I was a bunch of different things. I was an author—I'd fold a bunch of my dad's legal pad pages in half and staple them along the binding to make a book where I could write my stories. I was a teacher—I'd create versions of Spelling and Math worksheets by hand and give them to the neighborhood kids. I was a videographer—I'd come up with all these crazy ideas for "shows" that I could produce, whether it be modeling the latest clothes in fashion shows, stage plays with American Girl Dolls, or reports on the evening news about the local happenings in the neighborhood. I look back at all these things I *loved* to do as a kid—the things I would get lost in—and smile because it's transpired into my adult life.

I am an author because I write and publish books. I am a teacher because I'm a writing coach for aspiring authors. I am a videographer because I produce and edit YouTube videos.

As a kid, I *was* all of these things. And only now, as I've gotten older, do I realize that I've *always* been what I've *thought*—it just took jumping over a few hurdles and backtracking from some wrong turns to get here.

In addition, I had certain thoughts about myself when

I was a kid: *I am athletic, smart, a leader, and a light* in the community. This resulted in me being on every sports team imaginable while I was growing up, to acing my AP and Honors classes in high school and graduating with over a 4.0 GPA, to being on the executive board in a leadership role in my sorority in college, to being where I am today as a writing coach and author who just wants to help and guide people to reach their full potential and live beautiful, fulfilling lives. You *feel* your thoughts. You *feel* what you think. And so . . .

You are what you think.

I truly believe with every ounce of my being that our thoughts become our reality. When we tell ourselves something, visualize it, and repeat it over and over again, we instill the qualities of that thought/vision into our minds—it becomes embedded, in a way. Just like if you were to plant a seed, you want to plant positive thoughts, nurture them, and watch them bloom—one by one—into a beautiful garden.

While this is great for positive thoughts, it also, unfortunately, works for negative thoughts. When we focus on the negative and tell ourselves harmful things, we're again planting a seed and nurturing it to eventually grow and develop. This may sound crazy, but I remember for about eight months feeling down on myself and feeling lethargic and tired while binge-watching episodes of Grey's Anatomy. And while I love that show, it wasn't the best thing, at the time, for my emotional and mental state. I remember watching some of the episodes and hearing some of the symptoms of the patients and thinking, "Huh, I feel that way sometimes." These negative thoughts of worry and fear festered (along with many other factors) and ultimately contributed to something actually going wrong with my health where I had to go under the knife, which I shared in chapter one.

I am convinced that my mindset, and the thoughts I was thinking at the time, greatly contributed to my health issues. I've read jaw-dropping stories in *The Secret* and other science journals of people in hospitals healing themselves of illnesses, curing themselves of cancer, and reclaiming their sight through mere mindset shifts. I know it sounds like I've taken a seat on the crazy-train, but *this is how powerful our minds actually are*. By the way, while we're on the topic, if you haven't read *The Secret*, I highly recommend it.

It's been some time since that "health scare", and in that time I have watched medical-trauma shows, but with one major adjustment: I shift my perspective *before* sitting down to watch them. I constantly remind myself that I am healthy and vibrant and strong, and that what I'm watching is merely just for educational purposes. I've been back to the doctor since then, once a year, and I'm as healthy as I've ever been.

You are what you think.

If you think you're unhappy, then your behavior will

reflect that. If you think you're overweight, then your outward appearance will reflect that. If you think you're lazy, then your actions will reflect that.

You are what you think.

In the grand scheme of things, life is way too short to be focusing on all the things we *don't* want to be. I don't know anyone who strives to be unhappy, overweight, or lazy. Do you? So why do we allow these types of thoughts to infiltrate our minds? Why do we waste precious time and energy focusing on them? They are simply *not true*, but the more we focus on them, and the more attention we give them, the truer they become and the more likely we are to manifest them into our lives.

If you're a perpetual negative thinker—and have been for most of your life—take heed in that it's going to be a much larger change for you than for someone who only has negative thoughts once in a blue moon. The next time you catch yourself thinking a negative thought, remember that the more you think it, the more likely it will eventually come to be. Instead, pull out a journal and complete the following exercises:

BYOG ACTION 16: For five days straight, do the best you can to log as many negative thoughts that enter your mind. These thoughts normally start with, "I wish, "What if", "I should", "I don't", "I never" and "I can't". Then, there will be some thoughts hiding in plain sight like "I hate my thighs" or "My nose is too big" or "I'm so lazy".

Write down as many of these as you can catch while your mind is thinking them.

BYOG ACTION 17: At the end of the day, read over these negative thoughts and then write down how you spent the rest of your day. How did these thoughts affect your day? What did you do because of them? What didn't you do because of them? How did they hold you back? Did they carry over into the next day?

BYOG ACTION 18: Start fresh with a new day. When you start to think something negative about yourself or your situation, write down the thought, and then flip it to something positive. For example, if you catch yourself thinking about how much you hate your thighs, the positive thought would be: "I am so fortunate to have two working legs that allow me to walk, run, play, and dance." If you catch yourself thinking your nose is too big, the positive thought would be: "I am so grateful I have the means to breathe fresh air, smell fall-scented candles, and taste my food." Have you ever eaten something when you have a stuffy nose from a cold? You can't taste anything! Imagine if you didn't have your nose and could never taste food ever again. That would be downright cruel.

BYOG ACTION 19: The only way we can shift our

negative thoughts to positive ones is to become fully aware of *what* our negative thoughts *are* and how often we think them. By changing the quality of your thoughts and the frequency in which you think them, you'll allow yourself to rediscover the person you've always been—a positive, badass woman who goes for what she wants without fear of failing or concern for what other people think of her. *But,* since we are all human, and those negative thoughts will creep in every now and again, it takes daily practice and mindfulness to catch these thoughts. This step will likely always be a work-in-progress, and that's perfectly okay.

Closing Thought :

Your thoughts create your reality.

Positive thoughts, positive reality.

Negative thoughts, negative reality.

chapter five

NO MATTER WHAT you've been led to believe, time has never been your enemy—and there's always been more than enough of it to go around. The one phrase I undoubtedly hear the most is *I don't have time.*

Well, I hate to be the one to break it to you, but you *do* have time. You have 24 hours, which is 1,440 minutes, in every single day. For seven or eight of those hours, you may be sleeping, and another eight you may be working, which leaves us with eight full hours each and every day that you have *to yourself*—even if you have kids, a spouse, or other responsibilities—those eight hours are still *your* time and *you* get to choose what to do with it.

That's 480 minutes, folks.

The feeling of *not having enough time*, then, comes in when you've used up all of your **cognitive fuel**, as Mario Forleo puts it, which is the *real* good stuff—that brainpower you feel in the morning when you've had a restful night's sleep and you're ready to take on the day.

January 6, 2018. This was a day where I literally felt as though I should have won a Get-The-Most-Shit-Done award—if only such an award existed—because I flew through my to-do list as if it were my last day on this Earth. This date has been forever burned into my mind as my most productive day ever, and I actually have a post-it note stuck to my desk to remind me to **Live Everyday Like It's January 6th**. I also have this day earmarked in my planner so I can refer back to my insanely prolific timetable when I'm trying to remember how in the world I managed to do everything I'm about to share with you.

It was a Saturday morning, and in true early-bird fashion, I'd woken up at five o'clock. Unable to fall back asleep, I'd pulled myself out of bed, thrown my workout gear on, and went for a two-mile run. The weather had been just cool enough to need a light jacket, but warm enough to not sweat profusely from my pores, which, in my opinion, is the *perfect* running weather.

After my run, I'd fresh-squeezed some fruits and veggies for my green juice, meditated for ten minutes using the *Calm* app, wrote in my journal, showered, got ready, and filmed two videos for YouTube. I'd also managed to record a podcast episode.

Normally, in *everyday-Kristen-land,* this is a full day for me—but at the time I'd finished that last task, it was only 9:45 in the morning.

Nine. Forty. Five.

Since I'd woken up at 5 A.M., a solid four hours had gone by, but it hadn't felt like it—and seeing how much I'd achieved before lunchtime motivated me even more, so I'd decided to push myself even further, thinking, "How much more can I do today?"

A lot, apparently.

I continued on with my day to unload the dishwasher, wash, fold, *and* put away the laundry, vacuum the house, package some signed copies of books, stop by the post office, run to the grocery store, edit both of my videos, take some photos for Instagram, cook myself a healthy dinner, and write 800 words of my new book.

Pause for loud exhale.

I'd also managed to read for thirty minutes before bed, calling for lights out at 10:00 P.M., and when my head hit that pillow I was OUT.

Was January 6th an exhausting day? Yes.

Did I get a bit of a high whilst marking things off of my to-do list? Yep, slightly.

Is this type of routine sustainable? Probably not.

While it may not be sustainable to have over-the-top days like this—and burnout is a real thing—it did show me that I AM capable of wiping out my to-do list. I am capable of not wasting hours watching Netflix or scrolling through social media. I am capable of managing and prioritizing my time to the fullest extent and getting more done in a 24-hour time period than I ever thought possible.

In reverting to earlier in this chapter when we discussed cognitive fuel, I'd like to point out that I *started* my day with important activities—meaning I used my cognitive fuel wisely. I exercised, meditated, journaled, and created—and I did it all *before* lunchtime rolled around.

Oftentimes, we end up using all our cognitive fuel on stressful, unimportant, minutiae. Browsing social media, watching Netflix, answering emails, gossiping about a coworker or your boss and how nuts they're driving you this week—*all* of this takes up brainpower, your precious cognitive fuel.

In almost all of the personal development texts I've read, it's been recommended to start your mornings off by partaking in only *creative* and *important* things—and I could not agree more. January 6th is a testament to that.

Here are some ways you can start your days off and use that precious cognitive fuel wisely:

- Journal your thoughts instead of checking your Instagram feed or emails.

- Meditate to better connect with yourself and set

your intentions for the day.

- Listen to some music and get in the zone, creatively, even if it's only for thirty minutes.

- Flesh out a scene for your book.

- Write a poem.

- Sketch something or paint.

- Practice the piano.

- Read a book.

Just start your days off by doing *something creative*, something that you truly *enjoy*.

Since we only have a limited amount of cognitive fuel, it's imperative to use it wisely. This is where *prioritizing* comes into play. If you wake up in the morning, and check your social media feeds, then your emails, then realize *Oh crap! I need to get ready to go to work/school!*, and then rush into the shower, don't eat breakfast, fly out the door, forget your phone charger, kick yourself for forgetting said phone charger, and hit an ungodly amount of traffic—*all* of that takes up your cognitive fuel.

Which is *why*, when you get home from a long day, you

don't feel like doing anything except for marathoning The Bachelor or Real Housewives for four hours. Even then, you're still left with four beautiful hours to express yourself creatively . . . but, lo and behold, you're too tired, so it's off to bed at eight o'clock for you!

If this sounds like a typical day for you, then it's time to **shake that mind-numbing routine**, right here and now. Your habits of checking your email and your social media feeds, rushing to get ready, and heading out the door in a state of frenzy will be difficult to break because it's what you've been doing for so long. It's how you've been living your life. But difficult **does not mean** impossible.

First, you have to decide that you sincerely *want* to change your routine—that you want to spend your cognitive fuel on things that are actually important and will help you grow and move forward both personally and professionally. It's an active decision, and one you must make right now, in order for the next steps to work.

Next, you must decide what exactly you *want* to spend your time on. Do you love to write? Read? Practice yoga? Cook? Bake? Paint? Draw? Create? Volunteer? Travel? You may be thinking, "Kristen, how can I travel in the mornings when I have to get to work?" Well, technically you can't—but what you *can* do is spend some time on Pinterest gathering scenic photos of places that you'd like to visit, create a vision board, make a bucket list, and even start planning a trip, even without firm dates. You could also search for a new job, one that might allow you to travel more—or start mapping out your own business that would give you this kind of freedom you crave. You have to give yourself time to dream and time to play.

Think back to when you were a kid. If you're anything like me, time seemed to pass so much slower. I didn't even really think about time, because as a kid, you don't have responsibilities, and you just get to play. You get to play, create, dream, and with no limits. But then, we grow up, we become adults, and we lose that ability to play. To be silly. To dream big dreams. Responsibilities arise, and so do bills, and company functions, and family events, and work obligations, and blah, blah, blah. I'm here to remind you that you need to leave time to *play*. Pick up a long lost hobby, or discover a new one. We are creative, soulful human beings, and it's written within our DNA to dream and play.

Once you've decided what things you'd rather spend your time doing than checking emails and browsing social media, you must *make* time for them. Notice, once again, how I said *make time*, not find time. Time is never actually found because it's there all along. How you're *spending* your time—well, that's a different story.

In order to *make* time for these play-dream-create activities, first you have to know where your time is going. I find it easiest to take a blank piece of paper and write down every single thing I do in a day. I also write down about how much time I spend doing each of those things. Then, I'll circle the things I absolutely *have* to do—usually work obligations, sleeping, eating, etc. I'll take a look at all of my daily activities, and then rank them on a 1 to 5 scale, 1 being those things that don't light me up at all (i.e. time wasters or things I hate doing) and 5 being those things that really light me up and make me happy.

After doing this exercise, I discovered some very eye-opening things about myself and how I used to prioritize my time, like how when I would get home from work, I would spend two full hours (sometimes more) either watching Netflix or scrolling through social media to "unwind" from the day.

TWO. HOURS.

Now that I've become aware of how I spend my time, I'm able to do something about it. You can't make an adjustment if you don't know what it is you need to adjust! So now, when I get home from work, especially after a long day, I'll journal through my feelings instead—with the TV off. I find that by channeling my energy into something that makes me feel relaxed and productive at the same time, I'm more likely to pick up and continue that creative/productive streak into the evening.

Now, if it was an exceptionally hard day, and I really need to do something mindless, then sometimes I will turn on the TV—however, I always set a timer on my phone for thirty minutes. I make a pact with myself to only watch one 30-minute show, and then get up and pursue my passion aka creating content of some sort.

This will be difficult at first, because again, you are breaking up with a routine that's held true for you for many, many months—maybe even years. It's best to start small, and I've found that building *habits* is the best way to transform your routine. I have a habit tracker, similar to the one on the next page, where I write down all of the daily habits I want to implement, and then give myself a checkmark for each day that I complete them.

Scientific studies show that it takes 21 days to build a habit, so tracking what you do each day is **key**. And, once something becomes a habit, it'll become a part of your daily routine—something you'll naturally do every day, like brushing your teeth—and ultimately will allow you to live your best, most playful, most productive life.

HABIT TRACKER

BYOG ACTION 20: Make a list of all the ways you want to play. Do you want to take more walks/hikes and surround yourself in nature? Do you want to travel? Do you want to write a book? Do you want to explore your city?

BYOG ACTION 21: Make a list of all the habits you'd like to form to live a better, fuller life. My daily habit list includes: journaling, meditating, reading for at least 30 minutes, moving my body for at least 30 minutes, creating *something* for at least one hour, drinking eight glasses of water, and texting or calling a family member or friend.

BYOG ACTION 22: Take a look at any items in your daily routine that don't light you up (the ones you gave a 1 or 2, if you followed this chapter's exercises). Can you eliminate these items? Can you replace them with something that, instead, brings you joy? If you gave a 1 or 2 to your job, then it may be time to start looking for a new one, or create a side-hustle that you can eventually grow into a full-time business (that's what I did!)

BYOG ACTION 23: Just like the habit tracker, use a day-planner to track your movements and activities throughout the day. I use a color-coding system (orange for work, blue for my author platform, green for mental and physical health, pink for errands, bills, emails, yellow for events/travel, and purple for non-book-related projects), where, at the end of each day, I sit down and highlight all of my activities for the day in its designated color. This helps give a visual representation of how I'm spending my days, and if there's too much of one color (especially orange or pink), then I'll know I need to dial it back the next day, and make more time for blue, green, and purple activities.

Closing Thought :

How you spend your time

will determine *how* you live your life.

chapter six

MANIFESTATION REQUIRES ACTION

HAVE YOU EVER made a wish, whether it was on a shooting star, a prayer before bed, or blowing out your birthday candles as a child? I'm guessing the answer is probably yes. Heck, when the clock strikes 11:11, I still make a wish. It's not surprising that we've made, and continue to make, wishes—to put what we want out into the universe—in the hopes that it'll be returned to us in some fashion.

Now, have any of your wishes ever come true? I can count on both hands the number of times I've had wishes come true. Maybe they didn't always come to fruition in the timeframe I'd wanted, but at some point, they *did* happen.

I'm an incredibly visual person. Not only must I write down what I see for my life and my future, but I also need to create a visual representation. I've been making "dream boards", or as they're more commonly known now as "vision boards", since I was in middle school. Before the internet was a thing, I remember asking my mom to drive me to the nearest Barnes & Noble so I could pick out some magazines (does anyone remember Tiger Beat?), just to bring them home, flip through them once, and then cut out pictures of Hanson and The Backstreet Boys.

For real. This is not a drill!

Even though my little middle-school self was cutting out photos of hunky teenagers and adolescent guys, collaging them, and then putting them on my wall, it was still a vision board, just a different one for a different time in my life. When I was in middle school, I wanted a cute guy to notice me. Don't we all?

But now, as a woman who's lived through her twenties, my vision board looks *very* different. And for good reason!

The reason I bring this up is because, whether you believe it or not, creating vision boards is **manifestation in action**. By taking the time to find photos that represent your hopes, dreams, and desires and curating a well-thought out collage, you are sending a message to the universe that *these* are the things that you hope to have in your life. And by looking at it each and every day, you are reminding yourself of what you want, and subconsciously moving the chess pieces of your life in such a way that will get you closer and closer and closer, until you finally have or experience each of those things. I know because I've done it, and it continues to happen for me. I'm a huge, *huge* believer in vision boards, so if you haven't tried it yet, or think it's too woo-woo, give it a shot. I mean, what do you really have to lose anyway?

I've also found that written gratitude practices and daily affirmations are directly linked to manifestation in action. Every morning, I wake up and write ten things I'm grateful for in my journal—often times, it ends up being more—as well as some daily affirmations that I feel I need to focus on for that day. Both of these lists vary from day-to-day, but just to give you an idea as to what my typical gratitude list looks like:

1. My health
2. My family
3. My furbabies
4. Pursuing my passion
5. Meditation
6. Filtered water
7. The roof over my head
8. Cozy blankets
9. Fresh green juice
10. The interwebs

And some of my favorite affirmations include:
I am the architect of my life; I build its foundation and choose its contents.

I am guided in my every step by the Universe, which leads me toward what I know I must do.

I am brimming with energy and overflowing with joy.

My potential to succeed is infinite.

Everything I so desire is already here, right now.

Abundance and prosperity are my birthright.

Everything that is happening now is happening for my ultimate good.

Just like we discussed in chapter four, our thoughts are like food—the thoughts you feed your mind will create your perception of reality, and like attracts like. Negative thoughts, negative reality. Positive thoughts, positive reality. I cannot emphasize this enough. You know when you're having a bad day and all you can seem to focus on are the *many* things that are going wrong, only to feel like the amount of things going wrong ends up getting multiplied by a thousand? The same goes for positive thoughts. When we focus on the positive things in our lives, we create *more* positive things—more opportunities, more grace, and more enjoyment. Manifesting all starts with the mind.

But I think where many people struggle with manifestation is in the *truly believing* part. It's not enough to just say these affirmations, or rattle off what you're grateful for—when you say these things, when you put them out there . . . you have to truly *feel* them. Feel the weight of your words. Feel the meaning. There's a sort of activation that is required within your mindset and your soul to shift these "sayings" into "core beliefs". Only when you truly believe what you are saying—and *feel* it to be true within your bones—will you begin to witness manifestation in action.

A great example of this was when I was getting ready to launch my coaching program for writers called Valiance. It was a nerve-racking experience, but I knew, deep down that becoming a writing coach and helping and inspiring others to write their books was what I was meant to do. I *believed* it, a million and one percent. And so I spent a lot of money, time, and effort creating something that I *believed* would create value for others. I *invested* in myself and my future. I spent money I didn't have on CRM systems and my own business and success coach. I said no to events and outings in order to make time to work on this program. I stayed up until 2 A.M. many nights and went to my full-time job the next day, feeling exhausted, but knowing that my time had been well spent. I even wrote my resignation letter for my corporate job and dated it the day of the launch, all because I believed in this program so much and how dramatically it would change the quality of my life.

Fast forward to Valiance launch day, which was January 15, 2018. In less than one week, I more than *doubled* the **monthly** income I make from my corporate job. In other words, in just **seven days,** I made **double** what I usually make in a month. *This* is manifestation in action. *This* is putting out into the universe what I know to be true in my heart.

Your actions must line up
with your desires.

Which brings me to my next point. In order to get what you want and curate a beautiful life, you must behave and act as if you *already have it* at this very moment. This can be difficult to do, right? How can you *act* a certain way or *do* certain things if you don't have the financial means necessary to behave as though you "already have it"?

I get it, trust me. I totally understand the concern here. But this is where faith and your core beliefs *must* take the wheel. I'll give you an example. I didn't have the financial means readily available and accessible to go on my very first domestic book tour. I mean, going on a book tour, especially as a self-published author, is expensive. It can cost upwards of $3,000 between flights and hotels alone.

But it's something I've always dreamed of, ever since I was a little girl, to travel to different places, sign copies of *my* books, and meet and connect with fans and readers alike. It's something I had thought about a lot for the latter half of 2017, and I kept thinking to myself, "How can I make this work? I know I can do this. I want to do this. I believe I can do this. I **will** make this work."

Well, in January 2018, I said, "Screw the fear, doubts, worries, and concerns, I'm doing it! No matter what, I'll figure it out. I'll find a way to pay for it because I always do." And once I **made the decision,** something miraculous happened. That very next day, I got an email from American Express telling me that, due to my outstanding history with them, my credit line had been extended by $6,500 *and* the interest rate on those purchases for that specific line of credit for the next 6 months would be 0%.

Coincidence? **I think not**.

There was my financial means, right there, staring me in the face. **BOOM**. So I, of course, took it as the sign that it was, and started reaching out to bookstores and checking on flights and you know what? I booked every single one of my flights, to 7 different cities, that same day, *and* each one cost me less than $130. Each of my hotel stays? Less than $99 per night. And within a month, I had heard back from all of the venues (all bookstores, by the way) telling me that they'd love to have me and host my event. The whole she-bang cost me less than

$2,500 (in which I've already been able to pay off that credit card at 0% interest due to my belief in Valiance), and I'm pursuing a life-long dream I've had since I was six years old.

I CANNOT MAKE THIS SHIT UP.

As soon as you **make the decision**, and actually **make** it, not just "say" you're gonna make it, the universe will fall at your feet to guide you and help you manifest the things that *you need* in order to make said decision happen. I truly believe this because it's happened to me time and time again. I make the decision and, suddenly, as if a magic wand has been waved, everything I need becomes available to me.

That's the thing, though—everything you need to do x, y, and z is available to you *right now*. It's available to you **this very instant.** As soon as you activate the decision from *wanting* to "Okay, this is actually happening, I'm doing it no matter what", you'll be amazed at the things that show up for you, and the things that have been there for you *all along*.

BYOG ACTION 24: Write down in your journal the things that you most want to do, whether it's travel the world, write and publish a book, become a life coach, inspire people through the spoken word, etc.

BYOG ACTION 25: Next, write down what's holding you back. Lack of money? Fear of some sort? Lack of time? Judgment from others?

BYOG ACTION 26: At the top of the page, write:

"The universe wants me to succeed. The universe will provide for me. I believe in the universe and all it has to offer in guiding me to realize my dreams."

BYOG ACTION 27: Now choose *one* of the things on your list and ask yourself, "In a world where I had all the money, all the time, and all the confidence in the world, what actions would I be taking toward this goal? How would I be behaving?" And those actions, my friend, are what you need to be *doing* **right now**, and how you need to be *behaving* **right now**. Don't concern yourself with the *how*—the universe will take care of that. Just *do*. *That* is manifestation in action.

Closing Thought :

Manifestation requires activation.

Your actions and behavior *must*

line up with what you desire.

chapter seven

CHANNEL YOUR NATURAL
STATE OF FLOW

WHAT EXACTLY IS flow? You know those times where you get *so* into something—I mean *really* into something—and you work on it for hours and hours without even realizing that it's been, well, hours and hours?

I like to call this our *natural state of flow.*

There are windows of time where we feel most inspired, most productive, and most "in sync" with whatever it is we're working on. It's those rare, but treasured, times where we throw our responsibilities to the wind and write on our back patios for three hours straight; or shut down the Barnes & Noble on a Friday night (you party animal, you); or have the flight attendant kindly tap you on the shoulder with a gentle reminder to stow your laptop because, somehow, a five-hour flight feels like only 30 minutes have passed.

You better believe all of these *states of flow* have happened to me, and let me tell you something. All of these experiences have one major thing in common: I **held space** for creativity. I held space for inspiration. I created *an opening* for these things to find me. Just like when we spring-clean our closets and donate old shoes and clothes, we must also frequently declutter our minds to make room for fresh, new ideas. Whether this means taking a break from your day-to-day, going on vacation, switching up your surroundings and environment, or meditating, make sure you break up your routine every now and again to clear the old and welcome the new.

For those who have experienced being *in flow*, you're also probably really aware of when you're *not* in flow—when you sit down to work on something and, for the life of you, cannot seem to get anything done. The spark just isn't there. In the writing world, we call this "writer's block", but it's applicable to any creative endeavor—so let's call it a *creative block* instead.

Channeling your natural state of flow isn't about trying to *force* inspiration to find you—it's actually quite the opposite. When you try to force yourself to do something that you're "just not feeling", it can actually do more harm than good—not only to your creative projects, but also to your mindset and ego. Think about it: have you ever had such an **intense** creative block appear that, even after a week has passed, you end up recalling how that block made you feel and keep yourself from continuing on with your project?

Oh, right. I think we call that procrastination.

There have been more than a few times where I've had less-than-optimal writing sessions. I'm talking diddlysquat. A whopping 30 words. The words weren't flowing, my sentences weren't connecting, and my ideas were just plain awful. Ergo, I'd cursed the creative gods, slammed my laptop shut, and wandered into the living room to go do something that didn't require any creative energy (also known as a Netflix marathon). I'd figured it was just a bad day and that I'd get my creative streak back the following day.

Well, the next day rolled around, but not in the way I'd hoped. When I'd thought about sitting down to write my book, I'd had that nagging feeling that I was going to have another terrible writing session—that I wouldn't be able to get any words down (yet again), and that this horrible pattern would continue for weeks and I'd *never* finish writing this book.

Whoa, girl. Let's not get ahead of ourselves, here.

If you've had this happen before, then you know how debilitating it feels. Being paralyzed by fear—the fear of having "another bad day" —is no way to live your life.

And if you listen to this fear, you're only giving it the power to control you and the work that you do.

The biggest lesson I've learned is that **I cannot put expectations on the words I am about to write**. If they're bad, let them be bad. If they're good, let them be good. You can always rewrite a scene, chapter, or even half the book later on down the road—but by allowing your creative blocks to control your actions, mindset, your attitude, and ultimately, your output, you can kiss the hopes of channeling your natural state of flow goodbye.

Flow cannot exist in a world of fear. Flow cannot exist in a world of judgment. Flow cannot exist in a world of expectations. Fear, judgment, and expectations go hand in hand in hand—you're judging yourself before even sitting down to write, expecting that you'll have a bad writing day, and fearing that these bad writing days will continue. How can your natural state of flow survive, and better yet, *thrive,* in all that negativity? The simple answer is that it can't.

It'll drown, never to resurface again.

We don't want that.

Fear, judgment, and expectations are exceptionally dangerous because they *feed* the hungry, gaping mouth of procrastination—that deep dark abyss we're all a little too familiar with—more familiar than we'd like to be. When you fear something, you'll put off doing it. When you judge yourself for your work, you'll put off doing it. And when you put expectations on yourself or the work you're about to produce—you guessed it—you'll put off doing it.

Ah, procrastination, my old friend.

Put quite simply, the longer you wait to eat something to please your grumbling tummy, the less food you actually eat. Have you ever noticed that? When your eyes are bigger than your stomach? You're literally "starving" and order a plate of nachos, spinach dip, and a full-size entrée *and* dessert, only to eat *half of one* of the appetizers?

Yeah, it happens to the best of us.

Similarly, the longer you procrastinate, the less work you'll actually do when you finally decide to get started on your projects. The longer you wait, the harder it will be to build your appetite back up. Let's not make things harder on ourselves than they already are, okay? We'll talk about one of my favorite methodologies (in chapter fifteen) that I use regularly to help me conquer procrastination when it rears its ugly head.

If anything, channeling your natural state of flow is all about your mindset. I know, I know, here I go talking about mindset again, but hear me out. It is an absolute prerequisite that your mind is clear—a blank slate—because if it's riddled with doubt, comparison, or worry—once again, flow can't be present. So the first thing you need to do is to be aware of your current mindset before you sit down to work on a creative project. Is it open and free to just *be*? Or is it closed and imprisoned in fear? If you find it's the latter, I recommend taking some time to either a) journal out how you're feeling; b) meditate with either the HeadSpace or Calm app, or c) move your body for a half hour doing yoga, running, or strength training. For me personally, I've found that all of these things help lift my spirits and help clear my head when I'm feeling foggy or bogged down with limiting beliefs. Find what works for you.

Next, create your sanctuary—and by this, I mean prepare your creative environment. Before I sit down to work on anything, I always fill up a large mason jar with lemon water, wipe down and organize my desk, light a candle, and put some instrumental music on in the background. I leave my phone in the bedroom and turn the Wi-Fi off on my laptop—I don't allow any distractions to come into my space. Don't discredit the impact of ambience. Curating a pleasant atmosphere will help you feel relaxed, calm, and happy—and may even spark some desired inspiration.

Once my mind is clear and my space is prepped, it's time to get to work. Before I begin any of my creative projects, I always say to myself, "I will do the best that I can today. My best is always enough." I'll usually repeat this around three or four times, until it really sinks in. I know it sounds cheesy, but I must remind myself that I am not setting expectations on the work I'm about to do, and I'm not prejudging my work before I've even started.

By reminding myself that I am going to do my best and that my best is always enough, I'm open and ready to begin working.

These three habits have essentially turned into what I like to call my *flow routine*. I don't always feel it right away, but once I get started, I tend to get in the zone, and it's difficult for me to stop.

BYOG ACTION 28: In your journal, write down the things that help to clear your mind. It could be exercising, journaling, meditating, reading, playing with your furbabies/kids, talking to a loved one, listening to a podcast or jamming out to a certain music playlist, etc.

BYOG ACTION 29: Write down the things you need in your space before you begin a creative endeavor. Perhaps you enjoy having coffee/tea, snacks, your headphones, and being in pajamas. Maybe you enjoy working outdoors, listening to the waves crash against the shore, or having a view of the mountains. If this is difficult for you to figure out, think back to a time when you were most productive with a creative project. What were your surroundings? Write them down, and try to mimic them as best you can.

BYOG ACTION 30: Come up with a mantra or saying that feels good for you. I shared mine above, but if it doesn't feel right for you, create one that does.

Closing Thought :

You can't *force* creative flow,

but you can *channel* it.

chapter eight

BE A YES-WOMAN

HAVE YOU HEARD or seen the movie *Yes Man* starring Jim Carrey and Zooey Deschanel? First off, if you haven't, I'd highly recommend watching it.

The storyline follows a guy who is living an incredibly mediocre life. He's negative, pessimistic, and says *no* almost every chance he gets. He ends up going to a "Yes-Seminar", where the participants are challenged to say *yes* to everything that is presented to them for a certain amount of time (the point being that saying yes will have a profoundly positive impact on your life).

That's as much as I'll reveal about *Yes Man*, but I'm intentionally bringing it up because we're going to talk about the importance of saying *yes* and why it's critical in becoming your own **#goals**.

While I don't believe that we should say yes to *every single thing* that is presented to us (there is such a thing as burnout and we must protect our energy and time), saying yes *more* than you say no can radically change your life.

Saying yes to things is how you'll *gain new experiences* and *open new doors*. It's how you'll discover what you like and what you don't like. It's how you'll make mistakes and learn important lessons. It's how you'll take risks and quantum leaps and, ultimately, be tremendously rewarded.

Of course, what would this chapter be without a few examples from my own life? For the first one, let's go back about eight years. I had just graduated from college and, as any new grad would be, I was on the hunt for a corporate job to land a stable salary, a 401K, health insurance, and ideally, a bonus of some sort.

At the time, I was living in Arizona (I graduated from Arizona State in 2010 with my Bachelor's in Supply Chain Management), and I had applied to jobs in Arizona and California, and a few over on the east coast. I had no idea exactly where I wanted to go—but it became really clear really fast that I didn't want to live in Arizona anymore. It felt like my *old* life (my college life), and I wanted a fresh start—something new.

Out of nowhere, a company in Houston, TX (of all places) reached out to me with a great job opportunity— one that paid a high starting salary ($50K right out of school), plus health insurance, plus a 401K where the employer would match up to a 6% contribution (essentially free money!), a bonus, *and* they'd give me a relocation package since I'd have to move.

Umm . . . SIGN ME UP. No brainer, right?

So, even though I didn't know a soul, nor had I ever been to Texas before, I interviewed, got the job, and packed up my entire life into my Hyundai Tucson and drove 17 hours to start a life in a place I had zero knowledge about.

In a nutshell, I said **yes**. Even though I was scared out of my mind and had no idea what I was getting myself into, I still said *yes*. I said yes to a new place, a new job, new friends . . . an entirely new life.

Mind you, I was only 22 years old, but my desire for a new beginning *outweighed* my fears. It outweighed my **what-ifs**. I refused to create fear scenarios that could control me—things like . . .

What if it doesn't work out, and I hate the job?

What if I get fired and then have no family or friends to fall back on?

What if I end up all alone in this city I've never even been to before?

Nope. Don't do it. **Don't create fear scenarios for a situation that hasn't even happened yet.** It's pointless. It's pointless to worry, and worrying about something is basically praying for what you *don't* want to happen, so *don't do it.*

By saying yes to that opportunity, I jump-started my corporate career. Now, it's not the career I want anymore (we'll get to that in a minute), but it took me down a much-needed growth journey of getting promotion after promotion, getting hired by another company (one that paid for my Master's degree in full), excelling and getting promoted again, to a place where I was making more than six figures a year, with a great bonus, a company car, a company credit card, and the ability to design my schedule—essentially, a dream job, right?

Well . . . it *was.*

Before I go on, I want to point out that I do not regret a single step along my journey. Every decision I have made has ultimately led me to where I am today, living in a beautiful home on the lake, with my precious furbabies, and my passion for writing and content creation igniting my soul.

But, if I hadn't said yes to that opportunity to move to Houston . . . I'm not sure I'd be anywhere near where I am today. I don't know if I would have had the life-changing realizations I've had. I don't know *what* my life would look like. Because I said yes to something terrifying and risky, and potentially very lonely, I've gained *all of this*. I've gained the life I have right now—and I am 100% head-over-heels in love with it.

Great risk demands great reward. I truly believe the bigger you leap, the greater the reward. It's been true with every single risk I've taken—even if the reward isn't immediate or staring me right in the face—it always shows up, and usually at the most unexpected—and the most desirable—of times.

Another huge risk I said yes to? Deciding to write and self-publish my books. In 2014, I had a major realization that even though I had a six-figure income, a company car, a great bonus structure, and a company credit card, I wasn't *happy*. You may be thinking, "How? How could all of that not make you happy? People would kill for that type of situation."

And you know what? You're right. I can understand the confusion because I *used* to be one of those people—I had achieved what I thought was my *dream* at a very young age. But you see, there was one gargantuan problem: the work I was doing *wasn't lighting me up*.

I cannot stress enough the *importance* of pursuing your passions and the things that make you happy—otherwise, what is the point of living?

Seriously.

You may think that more money or the next promotion or a new car or whatever else may make you happier, but the hard truth is that this type of happiness is *fleeting*. It'll last for a few months, maybe a year, and then you'll be onto the next thing, and each time you achieve that **next level**, you'll be left wondering *why* that thing you worked so hard to achieve isn't bringing you happiness anymore.

I'm here to tell you that it's because **whatever it is you're currently doing is not your passion**. Your passion shouldn't feel like work because it's something you truly enjoy doing. You get immersed in it—you get *lost in it*. It's those times when you're in your natural state of flow and when you finally look at the clock, you realize three hours have gone by and that you really need to pee and you're starving having only eaten a bagel earlier that morning.

Whatever that *thing* is that makes you behave like the bionic woman (who needs food or water anyway?!), **that's** your passion. **That's** your calling. And **that's** the thing that will play a major role in making you feel happy and fulfilled.

Here I go, saying this again, but **true happiness comes from within**. I believe we have to do a lot of inner work to rid ourselves of our fear stories and negative self-talk. We must cultivate self-love in order to experience a perma-state of happiness. It takes practice and effort— like a muscle, continue to flex it and it'll stay.

I've found that self-love, gratitude, and pursuing your passion are three major keys to happiness and fulfillment. When you love what you're doing, it's easy to be happy.

When you love every aspect of yourself, it's easy to be happy. When you feel grateful for the air you breathe and the body your soul inhabits . . . it's easy to be happy.

The key commonality here is that you have to say YES to each and every one of these things (your passion, gratitude, and self-love) in order to see them work wonders in your life.

It's a *conscious decision*.

Every day, you have to say, "Yes, I love myself. I love every flaw, every imperfection. I don't judge myself or talk down to myself." You have to say, "Yes, I am grateful for my soul, my body, my mind, the air I breathe, the water I drink, my glorious, powerful mind, Mother Nature and all it provides." You have to say, "Yes, I will pursue my passion, the things that truly light me up, no matter what, because life is too damn short to spend one more second loathing my existence in a job I hate, a relationship I'm miserable in, or any other situation that is no longer serving me."

Of course, saying *yes* isn't always the easiest thing to do. Oftentimes, saying no is much easier because we then don't have to worry about potential consequences, or failing, or messing up. We get to stay *comfortable*.

I don't know about you, but if you're anything like me, I would *much rather* live my life taking risks and falling down over and over again, scraping my knees and bruising my elbows, than coasting along in Comfortsville.

Because **nothing ever happens in Comfortsville.**

It's the same thing, day in and day out. No change. Personally, my worst nightmare is waking up and living the same exact day over and over and over again.

Cue Twilight Zone music

What it really comes down to is that **yes** and **no** have two very simple meanings. Yes = growth, adventure, and learning, and No = stagnancy, lack, and complacency. We are not meant to stand still; we are meant to SOAR.

You can only SOAR if you say *YES*.

BYOG ACTION 31: Write down three things that you've said "no" to over the past six months or the past year. It can be something as big as a job promotion, or something as small as grabbing drinks with a friend, or declining a girls' trip because you had too much on your plate.

BYOG ACTION 32: Next to each one, write down *why* you said no. What was the driving force behind your decision? Were you just tired? Not in the mood? Or did something get under your skin? Was there something deeper there that maybe scared you a little?

BYOG ACTION 33: Now write down the positive things that *could* have happened had you originally said yes to those things instead of no. For example, perhaps a promotion you said no to (this does happen, especially if you're presented with something called a "lateral move" where it's more work and responsibility for only a slight bump in pay) could have led to another opportunity at another company where you'd get to do the kind of work you've always dreamed of doing. Perhaps you didn't realize it at the time, but the original promotion was a stepping-stone to help launch that next phase of your life. Perhaps if you had said yes to grabbing drinks with a friend, you would have networked and made contact with someone who could help you further your business, your career, or possibly, get involved romantically with. Perhaps if you had said yes to the girl's trip, you would have walked away with a new perspective on something, feeling refreshed, energized, and closer than ever to your friends whom you may have started to lose touch with. But by saying no, what did you do instead? You probably stayed home and watched TV. Don't get me wrong—we all need our downtime—but don't forget, we also need adventure and opportunity, too.

BYOG ACTION 34: The next time you have a decision to make and you're on the fence about it, take a few minutes to revisit this exercise. Write down all the things that *could* happen if you say yes to this opportunity. Do any of these potential outcomes excite you—like *really* excite you? If so, without putting expectations on the situation, say yes and see what happens, especially if all you have to lose is another night at home in front of the TV.

Closing Thought :

Say YES to living life, and watch

as the Universe trips over itself

to open new doors just for you.

chapter nine

C H A N G E . The only real constant in life.

There's a quote I absolutely love by Jenna Galbut that says:

> "Each new chapter of our lives requests an old part of us to fall and a new part of us to rise."

Not only is this quote beautifully worded, it's also painstakingly true. I am most reminded of the concept of change when I think about spring-cleaning, especially when tackling my closet. By March, it's filled to the brim with clothes that I haven't worn in months, shoes that have already gone out of style, and purses I've forgotten about that still have the tags on them. We've all heard the old adage "get rid of the old to make room for the new"—and that's exactly what change in our lives is all about, except on a much grander scale than our walk-in closets.

When our closets are overflowing with stuff, there isn't room for anything new. Just like in life, when our schedules are packed to the minute and our minds are crammed full of useless information and old ideas, we can't make room for anything *new*. In tandem with the last chapter, saying yes to new ideas, new opportunities, and *change* will lead you down a path of growth; whereas staying rooted in your old mindsets, habits, and routines will cause you to become a permanent resident of complacency and stagnancy in Comfortsville.

But just because we say *yes* to change doesn't always mean we're fully *embracing* it. No, *embracing it* is a whole other ballgame. You may find this confusing, thinking, "But if I say yes to something new and different, doesn't that mean I'm embracing it—that I'm *embracing change*?"

Not exactly. How many times have you said yes to something, only to find that you were distracted/not present/thinking about the 18 million other things on your to-do list and how you should be doing *those things* instead of whatever that other thing is?

Embracing change demands a high level of self-awareness. We have to be fully present during the change, see and understand it with an open heart and mind, and, if we decide it'll have a positive impact on our lives, carry that change over into our daily routines, habits, way of thinking, and way of life.

Ultimately, there are two major types of change that can happen in our lives: **the welcome and the unexpected**. We usually view unexpected change as "bad" change, because . . . well, we aren't expecting it. An expectation is really just a specific outcome you've placed on a certain situation. When that outcome doesn't play out like you'd originally imagined it would, it's easy to throw that situation into the "bad change" pile. Releasing expectations is a key component of embracing change.

Let's say you go on a trip with some friends. Most likely, before you leave, you've envisioned in your head what you imagine the trip will be like. Perhaps you imagine going out to bars and clubs with your friends and dancing wildly like you did in your college days; or perhaps it's the polar opposite, where it's just a low-key weekend sitting on the beach, catching up, and chatting about life and love.

In either case, you're setting up expectations around your trip whether you realize it or not. So it's no wonder you're kind of upset when you arrive and Susan's locked herself in the bathroom, fighting with her boyfriend on the phone; Sara's already passed out, snoring, because she's exhausted from jet lag; and Sally's got her laptop all hooked up, about to hop on a conference call even though it's a Friday afternoon and she's been preapproved by her boss for her vacation.

It's easy to be *disappointed* because your expectations aren't matching up with reality.

However, if you just let things unfold naturally (how they're going to happen anyway), you may find yourself sitting on the beach with a strawberry daiquiri, looking out at the waves, feeling grateful, happy and not the least bit upset. Eventually, your friends will come join you when they're ready and you'll catch up and chat and end up having a great time. While this is a very minor example of embracing change, I've learned that instead of trying to control situations and force them to "turn out" a certain way—just sit back and allow them to unfold exactly the way they're meant to.

An unexpected change that springs to mind, front and center, is when I was sixteen years old and my parents divorced. As an already hormonal teenager about to graduate from high school, you can imagine this unexpected news ripped me apart from the inside out. I remember darting to the bathroom with my sister and locking ourselves inside, holding each other and sobbing because our lives would never be the same. It took some time (and a lot of goading) to get us to finally unlock the door.

Divorce is hard for anyone, at any age, but for two

hormonal teenage girls whose parents were high school sweethearts? It felt as though our world was ending. We couldn't even begin to fathom what we were about to face. We hated what was happening, and we couldn't wrap our heads around it. The family unit we'd grown to depend on was crumbling right before our very eyes.

Not surprisingly, things weren't easy in the years that followed. My father moved out. The house went on the market. My mother, sister, and I moved into a new house. I painted my bedroom a cotton-candy-pink because, apparently, I was having an adolescent-life-crisis before heading off to college.

Adjusting to a new life without my parents together was hard. Over the years, I felt myself growing jaded and bitter when it came to love. I built walls around my heart, refusing to let anyone in, because I was so terrified of ever experiencing those feelings again. Trusting others became a daily struggle, and both my mental and physical health suffered from it.

I made poor choices when I went off to college. My freshman year was a blur of alcohol, fraternity parties, and purging Taco Bell at two o'clock in the morning. Somehow, I managed to keep my GPA over a 3.5 and maintain my status as an Honors student, but I was not what you would call "healthy" in the slightest. I developed an eating disorder (bulimia nervosa) where I'd go to class (hungover), eat very little throughout the day, drink heavily at parties at night, binge-eat pizza, purge, pass out, and wake up only to repeat the same vicious cycle.

It may seem like I'm blaming this destructive behavior on my parents' divorce, but I'm not. Growing up in a strict household, I imagine I'd still go a little buck-wild in college, divorce or not. However, I *do* think it played a part in the *level* of the self-destructive path I was on. Those four years in college were some of the best times of my life, but they were also some of the most confusing. Having two different Thanksgivings and Christmases at two different houses (like we still do to this day) hasn't grown any easier—it's just grown to feel a little more normal. Calling my mom and then calling a separate number to talk to my dad doesn't feel weird or bad—just different. Watching old videotapes of my sister and me as babies still triggers reminders of what once was, but I've come to terms with how things are now.

Fast-forward to the present where my parents are both happily remarried and continue to move forward with their lives. I visit as regularly as I can (as much as my vacation time will allow), and truly enjoy every moment I spend with my family—even if it's not *exactly* in the way I'd pictured it as a kid. Seeing their current relationships, I believe they've both found someone who is better suited to their personalities—someone who brings out the best and most loving side of each of them.

My sixteen-year-old self never could have seen the

potential for a happy ending. A happy ending wasn't even on the radar. Even though I resisted this change for many, many years, I eventually learned to embrace it. I also had to learn to not hold a grudge, to not *need* to understand why, and to not place blame or point fingers at anyone.

Change is no one person's fault. Sometimes things just happen. Feelings change, situations change, and experiences change. Some people grow together; others grow apart. Some people enter your life forever; others only for a season. How you choose to perceive a situation may also change. Sixteen-year-old me perceived my parents' divorce as an unwelcome, unexpected change. More than a decade later, I now perceive this change as necessary—necessary for the health and happiness of my mother, father, sister, and me. We've also welcomed two wonderful people into our family—my mom's husband and my dad's wife—whom I've formed special bonds with and couldn't imagine life without.

Enough about unexpected changes, let's talk about *welcome* changes. Welcome changes are the things we get excited about, and usually involve things like promotions, engagements, marriages, graduations, growing your family, moves, vacations, and retirement. These are *welcome* changes because they're usually something we've decided **we want** at some point or another. It's all in how we view the situation at hand.

Take moving, for instance. Moving can either be a

very welcome change, or it can be an unexpected one. If you've had your mind set on moving for a while and you've been traveling to different cities and apartment/house shopping, then moving will likely be a welcome change for you. On the other hand, if you get a promotion (welcome change) but then find out that it will require you to move to a completely different state (unexpected change), suddenly you may view this experience as being bad instead of good. You weren't *expecting* the move, just the promotion. So it makes sense for you to be upset and thrown off your game, right? Instead of freaking out and panicking about this giant decision that's been thrown at you, curveball-style, take a moment to think about *why* this is happening. Have you secretly always wanted to move, but have been too afraid to break your tight-knit family's hearts? Or, on the other end of the spectrum, did you perhaps *think* you wanted this promotion, when the reality is that the workload will double and the pay is still somewhat dismal? Perhaps this unexpected change is actually a welcome change in disguise or vice versa.

As I mentioned in previous chapters, after I graduated from college, I was offered a job in Texas that I hadn't even applied for. It was completely unexpected, but I didn't view it as a "bad" change—just **a** change. I knew I wanted to move away from Arizona, I just didn't know where, and honestly, Texas, hadn't even been on my radar. But the job sounded promising, so I decided to call the recruiter back and get more information. Lo and behold, it was everything I was looking for to start my career. I embraced the opportunity—this idea of *change*—and allowed it to guide me. Because I embraced this unexpected change, I now live a beautiful life where I am happy, financially secure, in a beautiful home, with my wonderful furbabies, pursuing my passion on a daily basis.

Speaking of, *that* was another unexpected change I had to embrace: the realization that even with the great salary, bonus structure, company car, and company credit card, I still didn't feel fulfilled. I wasn't happy. That was a tough pill to swallow because I felt as though everything I had worked for my whole life was a giant waste of time and energy. All that effort, all those hours . . . but you know what? They weren't a waste of time because those experiences taught me exactly what I needed to know. My experience in the corporate world made me realize that *I don't want* to work in the corporate world. It also made me savvy enough and helped me feel confident enough to start my own business, to pursue my passion, to truly understand what it would take to make money as a creative entrepreneur. If I hadn't embraced each of these changes during these different seasons of my life, I wouldn't be where I am today. Everything that has happened in my life has led me to this point. And I know those last two sentences are probably reminiscent of every personal development book you've ever read, but that's because *it's the truth*.

Embracing change doesn't just mean saying yes to something—it means bucking up and going for it. It's the understanding that life is going to throw you welcome changes and unexpected changes, and that the only difference between the two is what expectations you've previously put on the outcome of your life.

Release expectations, invite opportunity. Exhale specific outcomes, inhale flow.

Willingly open your mind to see the good in change and embrace it wholeheartedly. Accept it and don't try to change *change* because it's happening for a reason. Those reasons may not be clear right now, but eventually they will be, and sooner than you might think.

BYOG ACTION 35: Write down three *welcome* changes that have occurred in your life. Then write in what ways they've impacted you, whether good or bad.

BYOG ACTION 36: Now write down three unexpected changes that have occurred in your life, maybe even ones that are occurring right now. If they occurred in the past, note whether or not you embraced those changes or if you resisted them. What ended up happening? Did that change happen anyway? If it's a present-day unexpected change, write down the potential *good* that could come out of this situation. If it's a situation where it seems like there is absolutely no good that could come from it, like the death of a loved one, reflect and write down what you learned from that person. What did they teach you? What did you learn from them? What will you honor in them and carry with you and spread to others? How can you keep their spirit and their teachings alive?

BYOG ACTION 37: The next time you are faced with an unexpected change, revisit this exercise. If the change feels "bad" in any way, get to the root as to *why*. Every time change rears its head, we will experience both rewards and consequences, good and bad. It's the yin and the yang of life. But how you choose to *perceive* the change is what will ultimately turn an unexpected change into a welcome one.

Closing Thought :

"Your life does not get better by chance,

it gets better by change."

–Jim Rohn

chapter ten

LEVEL WITH YOUR SELF-DOUBT

I'LL JUST SAY IT.

Self-doubt blows.

No matter who you are—whether you're Tony Robbins, Oprah, or Ghandi—we've all faced self-doubt at one point or another.

I've always imagined self-doubt as a miniature troll living under a bridge—the bridge being our mind. The troll just sits there and sits there, sometimes sleeping, until BAM! Something wakes it and it starts swinging its stupid club around, making detrimental contact to the bridge, slowly trying to wear it down until it collapses and crumbles. The troll is potentially harmless until something activates it, where it then decides to wreak havoc and destroy everything in its path.

And it's always a snowball effect, right? One limiting thought leads to another and another until eventually you're left in a black pit of *I'm not good enough* and *I suck at life*. Not a fun place to be in, let me tell you.

If you've ever experienced self-doubt, then you're probably wide-eyed and nodding your head right now because you *know* this feeling—and it sucks. You are fully aware that you have your own troll living in the deepest, darkest depths of your mind, and that no matter what you try to do to squash it, it will always remain.

It may take a troll-vacation for a couple of weeks—months, maybe—but it *always* comes back. And, the majority of the time, it comes back bigger and more forceful than ever, swinging its club back and forth, damaging even more of the bridge than before.

If I've learned anything during this spiritual journey I've been on for the last two years, it's that self-doubt, anxiety, worry, and fear never truly go away, nor would we want them to. It's part of human nature to experience these emotions, and for good reason.

That little voice in your head telling you not to touch a hot stove or to put your seatbelt on when you get into the car is there for a reason—to protect you and to keep you from getting hurt. These thoughts do stem from fear, so in a sense, some fear is needed in our lives so that we don't suddenly decide to throw on a cape and catapult ourselves off the roof because Superman did it and he turned out just fine.

Where fear becomes an issue is when it paralyzes us from moving forward, from trying new things, from *experiencing* life. Sadly, that annoying little troll plays a **huge** part in whether or not we actually live life to its fullest potential, or settle in fear and just get by.

Seeds of self-doubt are planted within us from a very early age, especially as females. We're told to look a certain way (pretty), behave a certain way (nice), dress a certain way (conservative), and talk a certain way (proper). These planted seeds then become truths, or agreements, that we make with ourselves—a sort of covenant, if you will. When we stray from these truths, these *agreements*, we begin to question ourselves, which then opens up space for other people to question us. Society begins to scold us, and likely, attempts more than once to humiliate us.

So it's no wonder that self-doubt creeps in.

Having these **untrue** truths solidified in your life as a child makes it almost impossible to examine them and flip them around the older we get. Your worth is not determined by how you look on the outside. It's not determined by how you dress. It's not determined by your behavior or the words you speak.

Your worth comes from within.

Your worth comes from your *soul*, who you are at your core. That little voice that rises up when you witness injustice and decide to do something about it, or when you experience kindness and suddenly want to open the door for everyone and smile at strangers because it *feels* good—in those very moments, that's your *soul* that is emerging. Your moral compass guides your soul, which is how we know right from wrong, good from bad. It's why we speak up when someone is being bullied or lend a shoulder to cry on when someone is hurting.

Your *soul* is the thing that makes you *you*. No one will ever have the exact same experiences as you, see the world through the same lens as you, have the exact same thought processes as you—and so your worth and your soul are intimately connected, because without one, the other cannot exist.

Had I been taught this at an early age, I probably wouldn't have gone on insane diets, bleached my hair, bought different color contacts, worn clothes I didn't feel comfortable in, stayed in toxic relationships, and pursued a degree I had zero interest in, ultimately transforming my beautiful, unique self to the mindless, numb drone that society had convinced me to become.

By influencing kids at an early age to be or act or dress a certain way—by questioning their *worth*—we're suppressing who they are **as individuals**.

Of course, this is exactly what society wants, right? Fit in. Don't be different. Fake it 'til you make it. Do what everyone else is doing.

Live a miserable existence making money for the man,

where you'll eventually be laying on your death bed asking the one question that I'm sure haunts many into their afterlife: **"What the fuck was the point?"**

The *point* is TO LIVE.

Not to work your life away in a miserable existence making millions of dollars for some other person who doesn't give a shit about you—who doesn't even know your NAME—so that he can live the fabulous life YOU should be living.

FUCK. THAT.

And the old me would say "Apologies for my language" because society tells me it's un-ladylike to swear, but NOPE, not today, not whilst writing this chapter. If I have a point I'm trying to get across, I'm going to use my **individual expression**—including whatever expletives I need to do so—*especially* if it's going to wake up someone out there who's currently living the mediocre existence I was once living—and worse, blithely unaware of!

Nothing riles me up more. This is something I am crazy-passionate about and I've made it my life's mission to shake people awake—which is why and how my podcast and this book were born.

It makes my blood boil just thinking about how many people out there are living crappy, mediocre existences, *questioning their worth* on a daily basis, just barely scraping by, and SETTLING, because they've had the individuality beaten out of them by the time they were five years old and can't even follow their inner compass anymore, let alone find it!

It is *heartbreaking*.

It is a full-fledged **tragedy**.

I'm here to tell you that individuality IS beautiful. Self-expression IS the way of the future. Your thoughts, your opinions, your perspectives, your experiences—these are all unique TO YOU, and whether you believe it or not, you have gifts, talents, and a voice that this world NEEDS.

So, how can we express ourselves in a world of *be this* and *do that?* How do we find our way back to our true selves after being lost our whole lives?

I've found that when self-doubt creeps in, it's a reminder that what I'm doing scares the living shit out of me, which means that it's probably *exactly* what I should be doing. (Ha! How backwards is that?)

But think about it in the sense of that stupid little troll taunting you—telling you that you're *not good enough*, that you're *worthless*, that you're not *as good* as this person or that person, that you'll *never make a difference* in this world, that you're **boring, average, and mediocre**—you wouldn't (and shouldn't) take that shit! That troll is WRONG.

Bye-bye, troll! You don't know what you're talking about, so you can simmer in your own festering stew of doubts and leave me the hell alone so I can go fearlessly on my way to living the life I've always known I deserved.

Now is the time to *flip the script* on your self-doubt, on that ignorant little troll. If you want to write a book or release a collection of poems out into the world, but you're terrified of what your family and friends will think—that's the troll talking. If you want to become a musician who travels the world and lives life on the road, but you're afraid of being judged or ridiculed—that's the troll talking. If you want to attend culinary school and live your own version of *Julie & Julia*, but the thought of going into debt over a "nontraditional path" makes you cringe—that's the troll talking.

Do not listen to the troll. The troll is stupid.

How does that quote go? You only miss 100% of the chances you don't take? If you don't at least *try*, you'll never know what could be. Your family and friends may support you; they may not. You may be judged or ridiculed; or you may not. You may go into debt . . . or maybe you'll receive a grant or scholarship.

Wouldn't that be grand?

At the very least, if you don't the risk, you'll **never know.** Moreover, who *really* cares what other people think? Is it *their* life? Nope. Last I checked, it's **yours.**

Seriously. WHO CARES?

You don't need anyone's permission. You don't need anyone's blessing. No one else is living your life but YOU, so if writing and spreading your message is what YOU want to do, then **do it.** If playing on a cross-country music tour is your dream, then **do it**. If learning to cook the perfect beef bourguignon will make your teenage self smile, then **do it.**

Your happiness is all that matters. So long as you're not physically harming anyone, **you do you**, boo.

BYOG ACTION 38: Make a list of three scenarios where you've experienced self-doubt, but went through with it anyway. Maybe it was applying or interviewing for a job, auditioning for a role in a play, starting to write a book, or joining a club or organization.

BYOG ACTION 39: Next to each one, write down the specific doubt you had for each scenario. So if you were interviewing or auditioning for something, perhaps you doubted your preparedness. If you started writing a book, perhaps you doubted your ability to write well. If you joined a club or organization, perhaps you doubted your ability to make new friends and socialize with strangers.

BYOG ACTION 40: Now write down what *fear* that doubt stemmed from. Was it fear of failure? Fear of unacceptance? Fear of judgment? Fear of lack or not having enough? If needed, go back to chapter one and review sub-section three, as well as the BYOG actions there.

BYOG ACTION 41: Most likely, you've found that self-doubt and fear of *something* are directly linked. We doubt our abilities and ourselves because we are *afraid* of something. Take some time to write down the absolute *worst* thing that could have happened in each scenario had that fear come true.

So, for an audition of sorts, the fear was probably of failure and/or judgment—so the worst-case scenario is not getting the role you went for because you weren't "good enough" or "right" for the part—meaning you'd just have to start over, look for a new role, and try again.

But, for some reason, our silly little minds tend to blow things out of proportion, where the worst case scenario becomes being laughed off stage and the director calling all of his director-friends and telling them not to hire you, which would result in you being out of work for months, living on the streets in a cardboard box, eating scraps and developing a drug addiction. Let's be realistic. Which is more likely—that you fail and try again, or fail and suddenly become a drug addict?

If we allow it to, self-doubt and fear can snowball into unlikely scenarios. The next time you start to doubt yourself, write down the worst-case scenario. You'll gain some perspective and realize just how creative your mind can be at coming up with these ridiculous, unrealistic, highly unlikely scenarios, and that what you're actually afraid of . . . really isn't that scary after all.

Closing Thought :

Express your truest self, for it

is the way of the future.

chapter eleven

FLEE FROM THE COMPARISON TRAP

COMPARISON IS THE thief of joy—a quote we've all heard time and time again—and yet, you've probably found, just like me, that you've caught yourself (or still catch yourself) comparing your journey, life, relationship, experiences—whatever it may be—to others'.

I've already mentioned in previous chapters my need for acceptance and to feel as though I "fit in" when I was in middle school and high school—seven years of my life wasted and misused comparing myself to those around me, instead of focusing on myself and everything I had to offer. I was young then, and I'm sure maturity played a large role in being caught in the comparison trap, but even to this day, I still catch myself, every once in a while, looking at what other people are doing, asking if I'm doing enough—if, perhaps, I should be doing more?

One of the most important lessons I've learned in life is to *stay in your own lane*. Just like driving in traffic, this metaphor applies to life.

Don't drift into other lanes = don't get so absorbed in what other people are doing.

Focus on the road in front of you = focus on your own stuff at your own speed and trust the timing of the Universe.

Every once in a while, you can check your rearview and side mirrors = it's okay to be *aware* of what other people are doing, but there's no need to get completely absorbed by it.

Stay in your own lane.

It's the key principle by which I live my life.

And let me tell you, it makes for an incredibly fulfilling and stress-free one.

As a creative entrepreneur and an author, it's so easy to get sucked into what other people are doing. Thoughts like . . .

So-and-so created a YouTube channel? I should, too.

So-and-so made special gifts for their pre-order campaign for their book? I should offer my readers more.

So-and-so writes books in one month? I should really up my game.

*So-and-so creates this type of content and has this many followers so that must be **exactly** the path I should take . . .*

All I hear is *should, should, should.* What *should* you do to start, to grow, to become better, to *win?* **Should** is a dangerous concept when it's not aligned with your truth. The fact of the matter is there is no **one set path** to become successful or to "win" at whatever it is you want to do or become.

I promise you, **we're all just making it up as we go.**

No one handed me a guidebook for becoming a creative entrepreneur who writes books, records podcasts, films YouTube videos, creates webinars and launches coaching programs—these ideas all came from my own noggin.

Did I reach out to mentors and business and success coaches along the way? Absolutely! It's pointless to reinvent the wheel—not to mention it's a waste of time and energy (which are two things we obviously want to preserve)—but when I first started out, what I *didn't* do was look to what everyone *else* was doing and say, "Oh, I should do that, too."

I started a YouTube channel because *I* wanted to. I make writing advice videos and day-in-the-life vlogs because *I* want to. I started a podcast because *I* wanted a separate platform for my personal development content. Everything I've done in my business, every action I've taken, has been *for me, by me,* because I could see the bigger picture and how it would fit together in this giant enigma that is Kristen Martin Books, Black Falcon Press, and That Smart Hustle.

It's also exactly the reason why I've said no to different business opportunities. For example, when I first started my publishing company, Black Falcon Press, I originally thought I wanted to be a small publisher—meaning I would accept submissions from other indie authors and publish their work for them under my publishing company's name. It seemed like a logical next step.

But after doing tons of research and making multiple pros and cons lists, I quickly realized that I didn't *want* to do this. I didn't want to act as a literary agent, a publisher, and a marketer for other writers—I only wanted to do that for myself. Had I decided to go down this route, the amount of time I would have spent reading query letters, editing and formatting manuscripts to get them ready for publication, and marketing others' books, would have left me with ZERO time to write my own books and create content—which is all I *really* want to do.

So, I had to tweak my business model to make it work for me *without* looking to what other people in my industry were doing. I know some authors who offer editing services, and that's great! At one point, I thought I wanted to do this, so I started small and offered first chapter critiques. After doing about four of them, I realized it just wasn't for me. I didn't enjoy editing others' work—again, because I am a *creator*. I live to create things, not edit something that's already there.

I digress. When it really comes down to it, comparison is just like a virus—it never actually goes away. Just like when you get a cold, the virus lingers, but never fully dies. Your body just learns how to cope with this latent virus and keeps it from attacking your throat, nose, and head.

It's human nature to want to feel accepted and loved—I mean, we stay in groups and huddle for warmth as a survival tactic. So of course there are going to be times where we compare ourselves to the gorgeous girl who just waltzed into the room with the on-point outfit, voluminous hair, flawless skin, and blindingly white teeth—the girl that appears to have her life fully together. Of course we're going to compare our own writing to those authors that we look up to. Of course we're going to compare our business to those who are doing something similar and are achieving insane amounts of success.

But instead of negatively comparing (*should, should should*) and getting in your own head, ask yourself what it is you can *learn* from this person. What are they doing or what do they have that you're interested in? More importantly, what are they doing or what do they have that you're *not* interested in?

I say this because no two paths are going to be the same. And why would you ever want them to be? Sure, the thought of having a step-by-step guide to creating your dream life sounds great, but where's the fun in that? If I had gotten a step-by-step guide, this book never would have been written because another book would have already existed. My journey would have been the same as someone else's. I don't want that. I don't want it for me, and I certainly don't want it for you.

Our experiences are unique to each and every one of us, and while you may find some similarities between your path and my own while reading this book, ultimately, no two journeys are the same. If you can find someone who's done what you want to do, it's okay to look for those similarities (and even ask for guidance/mentorship), but please, never ever compare your journey to someone else's. They are meant to be different. We've all had unique pasts and upbringings *for a reason*, and so the lessons I've learned along the way may be lessons you've already learned and vice versa—just like how some of these chapters may be life changing and others may be concepts you're already familiar with.

One lesson I learned way too late is to ask for help when I really need it. I was raised to be independent—to not *need* anyone—and while this mindset has benefited me in more ways than I can count, it's also hindered me from experiencing a lot of things and from moving forward in certain areas of my life.

Seeking out mentors and like-minded people to learn from **is not** a weakness. Asking for help doesn't mean you aren't strong—it just means that you're able to put your pride and ego aside because you *don't* know everything. You are not the be-all, end-all of knowledge. There is always something to learn, and if there's someone out there who can teach you and guide you, seek them out. *But,* for the love of all things holy, do not spend your time comparing your situation to another person's, envying what they have. Their situation is the way it is for a reason, and yours is, too. When you can grasp the concept that destinations may be similar but all paths aren't created equal, you'll find yourself in a state of learning instead of comparing.

Hands down, the best way to avoid falling into the comparison trap is to be clear on who you are and what you want out of your life. When you know who you are and what you want, you won't be so easily swayed to "do what everyone else is doing". You won't feel pressured to do things that don't feel right for you. You'll be more confident in the choices you make and the foot you put forward.

Similarly, you should also define what success means to you. The life of that girl modeling on Instagram, making hundreds of thousands of dollars a year, might seem incredibly appealing and glamorous, but if her definition of success is being able to freely travel the world on someone else's dime and yours is to have more free time with your kids . . . you may want to rethink what it is you want. These two definitions of success, while having the same underlying principle of "freedom of time", are vastly different.

You'll also notice that your definition of success will likely change over the years—and this is okay. As we grow, we change, so it makes sense that our definitions of success will shift the older we become and the wiser we get. For instance, my definition of success as a teenager was completely different than how I view success today. As a teenager, I had a very narrow view of success—get good grades so that I could get into a good college. I worked for hours on homework assignments, triple-checked my essays before handing them in, and enrolled in a number of AP classes. But once I graduated and started applying for colleges and got accepted, then what? My definition of success was more of a goal—a long-term goal that I'd configured into a definition because at the time, going to school and getting an education was all I knew.

College was more of the same, yet also different. Because I had been so studious in my high school years, I wanted to *experience* life and have fun, while still maintaining a good grade point average. I may have had a little too much fun because believe it or not, it was actually in college where I failed (got a D) for the first time ever—in my Statistics class. My definition of success in college was feeling balanced—having fun while also learning and prepping for my future. All in all, I ended up with a 3.3 GPA and landed a great job just two months after graduation.

Once in the corporate world, my definition of success shifted yet again. I told myself that whenever I was finally promoted to a managerial level, I would finally feel successful. Promotion after promotion came and went, and in April 2017, I was promoted to a management role. This was also during the time when I had been building my author platform and rediscovering my passion for writing books, creating content, and inspiring others to live their best lives. I quickly realized that my definition of success no longer fit this new path I saw myself venturing down. I didn't want to work for anyone else—I wanted to work for myself.

To be a creative entrepreneur.

My definition of success may look very different from

yours, but as I've grown older and have gotten to know myself better, I think this new definition of success will stick:

To be completely and utterly in love with every aspect of my life, and to feel fulfilled, passionate, and inspired every single day for the rest of my days on this Earth.

Because we're all at different stages and phases in our lives, it's pointless to try and compare our journeys to those of our friends, family members, and even strangers. Perhaps you're not moving as fast as you'd like, simply because your definition of success hasn't yet evolved to the next level. We all have different levels when it comes to skillsets, available resources, experiences, connections, networks, and financial situations. Just know that you have all the tools you need *right now* to at least get started, or to elevate if you've been pursuing your passion for a while. Start looking within instead of comparing, and I promise you, things will get a whole lot clearer, and a whole lot brighter.

BYOG ACTION 42: Make a list of people you admire who are doing the things you want to be doing or living the kind of life you want to live.

BYOG ACTION 43: There's a major difference between feeling inspired by someone, and feeling envious or jealous. Inspiration comes from a positive space, whereas jealousy comes from a negative one. Write an **X** next to the people who make you feel envious or jealous. If you follow them on social media, un-follow them. Trust me on this one. If seeing everything they're doing makes you feel down on yourself, stop following them! You're only adding stressors and negativity to your life—two things that will keep you stuck in the comparison trap.

BYOG ACTION 44: Now circle the people on your list who inspire and motivate you to be better, do better, and live better. Subscribe to their websites and newsletters. Send them an email. Check to see if they offer services or programs that can help elevate you, your life, or your business to the next level. Look to them for inspiration and positivity, *but*, (and this is really important), **do not** allow yourself to fall into an obsessive state. Keep it positive and light.

BYOG ACTION 45: Pick one or two of your "circles" and write down the qualities you share with this person. Did you both have a similar childhood? Family structure? Financial upbringing? Drive and ambition? Write down all the things you have in common with this person and whenever you feel yourself diving headfirst into comparison, reference this list. It'll remind you of all the amazing qualities you have (that are subsequently shared with someone you really admire), ultimately putting the focus back on the positive and back on *you*.

Closing Thought :

"We won't be distracted by comparison

if we are captivated with purpose."

–Bob Goff

chapter twelve

THERE'S A QUOTE by Emma Watson that I absolutely love that says, "Don't feel stupid if you don't like what everyone else pretends to love."

Ah, this could not ring more true! I adore Emma Watson for multiple reasons, not only because she's a phenomenal actress in Harry Potter, The Perks of Being a Wallflower, and every other movie she's taken a role in; it's also because she's a total girlboss and has a huge heart. As a philanthropist, she supports causes like HeForShe, UNIFEM, and Millennium Promise, just to name a few. Okay, I'll stop fan-girling now—but the one thing that sets Emma Watson apart from the rest is that she doesn't *pretend* to be someone she's not.

I think we can all learn something here.

Being genuinely happy with yourself means not pretending to like certain things just because everyone else does. It means not wasting your time hanging out with people who bring you down or think you're "weird" because you'd rather stay in bed reading a good book than go out, binge-drink, and wake up the next morning with no recollection of the night prior.

One thing I've pretended to be interested in almost my whole life is watching sports. Not *playing* sports (that was actually fun), but *watching*. For me, watching sports is the equivalent of bird-watching (no offense to you bird-watchers out there!)—it's a straight-up SNOOZEFEST. I've just never cared to watch people run around a field or court, chasing some ball to try to score against the other team. Just to be clear, I'm not saying there's anything wrong if you *like* watching sports—it's just not my cup of tea.

As I've been reflecting on my faux-enthusiasm for watching sports, I've realized that perhaps I pretended to like it for so long because I grew up in a basketball-centric family. My dad and his brothers, and almost all of my male cousins, played basketball at some point or another, so that's what my family grew up focusing on. To this day, it's still a major focus for my dad's side of the family. And that's totally fine, but I no longer feel guilty for not knowing the latest sports stats, or which player was traded to which team, and so on. If sports-talk pops up, I politely excuse myself and return to the conversation once it's died down.

Speaking of sports and my need to stop pretending, I clearly remember when the Astros played in the World Series in Fall 2017. Now, how would I know something like this, seeing as I'm not a regular sports-watcher? Because it's all anyone at my workplace talked about for the weeks leading up to it!

When the World Series finally ended and we all lugged ourselves to work the next morning, my colleagues, not surprisingly, asked me if I saw *how amazing that last game was*. And you know what I did? I simply shook my head and say, "No, but good for them." They looked at me like I was insane—*how can she not care that the Astros won the WORLD SERIES? What's wrong with her?!*

I could sense the judgment and criticism from a mile away. And again, the answer is simple. Watching sports and regularly keeping up with certain teams just doesn't interest me. I have other things I'd rather be doing with my time, like reading, writing, creating content, podcasting, and filming videos for my YouTube channel. That's what is *fun* for me and I *enjoy it*—so I'm not going to sit there and force myself to do/watch something I don't enjoy and pretend to like it for the sake of "fitting in" or being able to give my two-cents at work when someone brings up the outcome of the game.

Subsequently, I'm not going to waste my time trying to

explain myself to people who don't understand me in the first place, and can't seem to get onboard with what I'm doing with my life. I'd rather use that energy to focus on finding my *soultribe*—those incredibly supportive groups of people that totally get you, your vibe, your personality, your dreams, and who you are as a person.

Now I'm not saying that these people have to completely understand the vision you have for your life— they just need to be accepting and supportive. I've gone through a lot of different friendships throughout my life, and you know what? I don't regret a single one of them, because they all served a certain purpose during certain phases of my life. But holding onto a friendship or relationship that isn't benefitting both you and the other person? Nuh-uh, honey. More likely than not, it's time to say *adios* to that relationship.

So, how *do* we find our soultribe? I don't know about you, but this is something I struggled with for quite some time, especially moving from Arizona to Houston after graduating from college, entering the corporate world, and the rise of the internet and "virtual" friendships versus meeting people in real life. While it is harder nowadays to meet people in real life, the beautiful thing about the internet is that it allows us to meet and connect with people from all over the world that we wouldn't have met otherwise.

Due to my YouTube channel, I feel like I now have this amazing community of like-minded writers, girlbosses, and straight up hustlers, who understand exactly what I experience on a daily basis. I felt such a deep connection with them that I actually decided to host the very first AuthorTube Retreat at my home in April 2018. Seven incredible women made the time in their insanely hectic lives to fly to Houston to spend the weekend getting to know one another. I'd always known I'd been missing that feeling of "community", and I can proudly say that after that weekend, I don't feel so alone as a writer anymore. I feel like I walked away from that weekend with seven new best friends—seven soul sisters.

They understand the struggle of finding time after their jobs or being a mom to work on their side hustle—that one thing they're truly passionate about. They understand the many emotions that overwhelm you when you finally write *all* the words or have a breakthrough A-HA! moment in your plot. They understand the frustration and sadness when you get your first negative book review. They understand more about my world because they, too, are living in it.

Shout-out to Kaila, Anna, Kim, Vivien, Jessi, Mandi, and Natalia—if you're reading this, please know how grateful I am for each and every one of you!

And I don't want you to think that you can have **just one** soultribe. You can have more than one. I actually have three tribes: my family, my childhood friends, and my AuthorTubers. My AuthorTube tribe is there to support and cheer each other on as we accomplish our writing goals and fulfill our dreams of becoming career authors. My childhood friends help remind me of a time when life was fun and carefree, and to live each day as if it's my last. My family knows the deepest parts of who I am as a person, and so whenever I feel like I've lost my way or need to get grounded and centered again, I reach out to them. They know me at my core, and they always help to guide me back home. While each of these tribes serves a different purpose, they all have one thing in common: they accept me for who I am and support me, as well as the decisions I make, no matter what.

When it comes down to it, all we really want is to be **loved and accepted for who we truly are**. I've been friends with people in the past who made me doubt my own self-worth, who I'd play the negative-comparison-game with, who took advantage of me and my big heart, and who didn't accept me for the person I am.

Does this sound familiar? Is there anyone in your life right now that makes you feel down about yourself, or who drains your energy?

Finding your soultribe is certainly fun and exciting, but we can't forget that we have to *make room* for these new relationships. The not-so-easy part of finding your tribe is releasing the old toxic relationships in order to make room for the supportive, uplifting new ones.

A relationship in your life is toxic if it:

- causes unnecessary drama

- drains your energy

- makes you feel angry, irritated, or frustrated more often than not

- causes you to constantly compare yourself (and not in a good way)

- makes you question and doubt your worth, your abilities, and who you are at your core

Of course, there will be varying levels of toxicity for each relationship in your life, and ultimately you have to decide whether having *Person X* in your life is doing more harm than good.

I'll give you an example of a person in my life that I am no longer friends with. It was when I first moved to Texas after graduating from college, and in the beginning, the friendship was great. We worked together, so we were able to see each other every day, and we were both the same age, in the same "life phase" (except she was engaged and I was single), but even so, we were pretty consistent in making plans over the weekends. Things were fine and dandy for months, until this one pivotal moment occurred in our friendship: she decided to break off her engagement, and, at the same time, I started dating someone new. In a mere couple of weeks, we suddenly swapped places on the relationship scale. She actually knew the guy that I was dating, and we were all friends, so I didn't think this would be a problem.

Lordy was I wrong.

Because of her engagement's demise, she needed a friend more than ever. And boy was I there for her. Our weekend plans didn't change, seeing as I still hung out with her (even though I had a boyfriend and wanted to spend time with him every now and again)—if anything, I neglected my new relationship and spent *even more* time with her because I knew she had just gone through something traumatic. But, as I'm sure you can imagine, she'd make me feel guilty when we weren't hanging out.

Trying desperately to remedy the situation and manage my time between these two relationships better, I figured since she knew my boyfriend, we could all hang out together. When she and I needed our "friendship" time, we could branch off and do our own thing. This worked for a while until the unnecessary drama started to creep in. I began to feel like she was constantly comparing her own situation to mine, complaining that there were no good guys left, and questioning my relationship with my boyfriend in a way that made me doubt whether or not it was right for me.

At this point in our friendship, whenever she'd call or text, I'd feel nothing but frustration and irritation. Whenever I'd talk to her, I felt drained afterwards. I knew that our friendship had shifted into something that wasn't healthy anymore. It may have been benefitting her, but it certainly wasn't benefitting me. Our friendship had turned into a toxic wasteland that I no longer wanted to run amuck in.

Sadly, things continued on like this for months, and even though my gut was telling me to remove this person from my life, I couldn't seem to do it. She was my first friend in a new city. She was also a coworker, so I knew that "breaking up" with her would make things at work super awkward. I struggled with this choice for what felt like years; that is, until she did the one backstabbing thing that you **do not do** to a girlfriend.

She hooked up with my boyfriend.

Yeah, should have seen that one coming.

Needless to say, we're not friends anymore. It's unfortunate that it had to go *that far* for me to finally remove this person from my life. Deep down, I knew her insecurity and jealous tendencies would hurt me in the end—heck, she was hurting me the whole damn time!— but I held onto our friendship because I didn't want to confront the real issues. If I'd had the courage to do so when I first saw the writing on the wall, I would have saved myself a whole lot of heartache.

So, the moral of the story here is to surround yourself with positive people who support, accept, and love you. Seek them out online if you're having trouble meeting people in real life. That's what I did and I have never felt so much love and support in my entire life!

Life is way too short to have people drain you of your precious energy and gifts to the world. Don't allow negative people to extinguish your light—and if it feels like a relationship is heading south, don't delay in acting on what you know is the right thing to do. Cut ties. End it sooner rather than later. Trust me when I say that you'll be so, so happy you did.

BYOG ACTION 46: Make a list of the five people you spend the most time with or talk to the most. Underneath each name, in the left column, write down all of the positive aspects of your relationship. In the right column, list all of the negative aspects. We're essentially making a pros and cons list here.

BYOG ACTION 47: Are there any people on this list who have more items in the right column than the left? If so, it may be time to reevaluate this relationship, and either make an action plan to improve it, or remove it completely. Making yourself unavailable to listen to this person's drama and complaints, and establishing boundaries, are two great first steps in slowly phasing this person out of your life, if need be.

BYOG ACTION 48: Now make a list of the ideal qualities of the people you'd like to have in your #soultribe. These could be things like: go-getters, drive and ambition, loyalty, honesty, supportive, accepting, loving, shares similar interests, etc. Compare this list with the positive aspects of the five people you listed above. Do they fit the bill? Do they cover most, if not all, of the bases?

BYOG ACTION 49: During this exercise, you may come to the realization that the people you spend the most time with—the **key players** in your life—actually aren't fulfilling all of the things you desire in the relationships with those closest to you. And this is perfectly okay. People change. People grow at different speeds at different times. Just because one of your relationships has changed doesn't necessarily mean it's a "toxic" relationship—it just means that the current life-phase you're in is *different* than the one they're in. Just make sure you don't close yourself off to potentially new, great relationships. Perhaps you and your best friend have different interests now than you used to, and you want someone in your inner circle who likes the same things you do and understands your hobbies and interests. There's room for both relationships. There's a difference between writing off a relationship because it's toxic and simply giving one a break because things have shifted slightly.

Closing Thought :

You are the average of the five people

you spend the most time with, so

surround yourself with *light.*

chapter thirteen

UNDERSTAND YOUR MONEY MENTALITY

YOU MAY BE wondering why there's a money chapter in this book, and while it may seem a little out of place in a book about becoming your own #goals, I promise you it's not. Why? Because having an abundance of money and financial freedom is a goal for a lot of people out there, so understanding our money mentality is key.

For some reason, money—like sex—is such a taboo topic, and yet it's something we think about *constantly*. In a sense, it runs our lives and it's what makes the world go round.

But . . .

It's just a freakin' piece of paper. That's it.

Money is neither good nor bad—it just *is*. It is a *neutral* resource, a *tool*. To explain this more clearly, think about a hammer. It's a tool, right? What you choose to *do* with that hammer, though, is where the "good" and the "bad" come into play. You can either build something with said hammer, like a chair, a table, or a home. *Or,* if you so choose, you can destroy something with that same hammer, like smashing a picture of your ex into a thousand tiny pieces.

But let me ask you this—do you have ill feelings towards hammers? Do you think about hammers all the time, cursing it, wishing there were *more* hammers in your life?

No, of course not.

But, if I had to guess, you've probably had these thoughts surrounding money. Feeling like there's never enough, cursing it for disappearing into a never-ending stream of bills. Trust me, I've been there—in a complete state of desperation—freaking out about how I'm going to scrounge up the money for next month's payments.

But you know what?

Money has <u>always</u> found me, *especially* during the times I've needed it most. This is because, if you have an overarching belief in the Universe, in God, in the Divine, in Spirit—in *whatever* you want to call it—like I do, then you know, deep down, that you *are* and *always will be* **infinitely supported**. The Universe *wants* to see you succeed. It *wants* to see you thrive. It *wants* you to live your best life, and It's going to do *everything* in Its power to guide you to the right places and to provide you with the *neutral resources*—MONEY!—at the right time so that you can make your dreams happen.

This guidance and this love from the Universe is available to you *this very instant*, but if you constantly feel like your bank account is a spiraling abyss in which money arrives, never to be seen again (seriously, where did it all go?), then you need to shift gears and *reframe* how you think about money and what it means to you.

So how do we do this?

It all starts (and ends) with our money stories.

We've all grown up with money stories. Just like fear stories and agreements we may have unknowingly made with ourselves in our younger years, we also have stories surrounding money—and I'm guessing, if you're experiencing the abyss I talked about just a second ago, your view on money is somewhat negative. Whether it was your single mother raising you and your two brothers, telling you there was never enough and pinching every penny earned; or a teacher who drilled it into your head that going to college is the *only* way to make a decent living, we all have money stories that have stuck with us into adulthood. It's yet another *agreement* we've made with ourselves about how money *is* and how it *behaves*. They've become our steadfast truths about money—and that's just "the way it is".

It all stems back to the *law of attraction*. Like attracts like. High-vibe energy attracts high-vibe energy, and low-vibe energy attracts—you guessed it—low-vibe energy.

Have you ever noticed that when you feel desperate, overwhelmed, and focused on *the lack* of money, that only *more* "lack" seems to find you? You sit there at your computer, staring at your mountain of credit card debt, wondering how you're going to pay even the minimum payment this month when—CRAP ON A SPATULA!—an unexpected expense suddenly catapults into your life out of NOWHERE? Like your dog starts vomiting profusely and you have to rush them to the vet? Or it's the middle of summer, in June, in Texas, and suddenly your A/C goes kaput? Or you accidentally book a flight for the wrong weekend and the airline you booked it through *sucks* and forces you to pay a $200 change fee?

Yep, you better believe that every single one of these situations has happened to me, but you know what I realized after reflecting on my journal entries before these seemingly *catastrophic* events took place? That during that time, I had been in a state of worry, anxiety, overwhelm, and desperation regarding my financial situation—meaning I was focused on the LACK of money in my life.

Huh. You don't say.

Like attracts like.

When you constantly worry about the *lack* of

something, how does it stand to reason, then, that you can expect anything *but lack* to show up in your life? When I focus on the money I *don't have*, more situations show up in my life to *add* to the *lack*. When I focus on every *bad date* I've ever had, I attract more of the same into my life—immature, selfish boys (I'm purposely not using the word men here) who don't give a rat's ass about me. When I focus on the stress at my job, more stress and more pointless projects get dumped into my lap. Sound familiar?

What I'm trying to say is that if you focus on the lack of *things,* you'll attract more of that. So instead, focus on what *you want* with an abundance mindset, and watch the powers that be work overtime to get it for you.

By this logic, then, money is *energy.* Everything around us is made of energy. The air we breathe. The thoughts we think. The chair I'm sitting in to write this book. The money we spend.

It's *all* energy.

And when you expel your energy on good things (like exercising, volunteering, acts of kindness), that same level of high-vibe energy is returned back to you—oftentimes, tenfold. But when you expel energy on bad things (like involving yourself in drama/gossip, staying in toxic situations, talking down to yourself and others), then that same low-vibe energy is what you will continue to attract into your life.

Likewise, when we pay for things, an energetic exchange takes place. When you spend your money on *good* things, like investing in your life or business to help it grow and make it better, more money will find its way to you, because you're using this *neutral resource*, this *tool,* for good. But, if you're blowing your hard-earned cash on booze, cigarettes, and another pair of shoes you don't need—well, you can do the math.

To this day, the best money I've ever spent was $2,000 on a business-and-success coach. And believe me, at the time, I did not have even *two nickels* to rub together. I was in thousands of dollars in credit card debt, student loan debt, and I hadn't gotten a raise (one I deserved, at least) in two years. But I'd found this girl online that I **immediately** connected with. She inspired me and motivated me, and there was something she'd figured out that I hadn't yet—how to make passive income through an online business.

I remember reading her story on her website and being moved to tears because I felt as though I were reading my own life struggles. We had some fundamental differences (seeing as she's happily married with kids), but the looming credit card debt and desire for freedom of time, money, and to make my schedule my own? Ding ding ding! Rang all my bells.

So, what did I do? I grabbed one of my "for emergencies only" credit cards (the only one that wasn't maxed out at the time) and purchased her TWO-

THOUSAND DOLLAR coaching program. In the months that followed, I worked my tail off to create a webinar series for aspiring entrepreneurs (Hustle Smarter, Not Harder), as well as my own online coaching program, specifically aimed at writers, called Valiance.

And guess what?

In half a year, I'd earned _over tenfold_ what her coaching program had cost me.

Ahem, that's a pretty **phenomenal** return on investment, if I do say so myself. Most people would have told me I was **insane** to spend that much money on a coaching program when I still had credit card bills to pay. But I didn't look at it that way.

By _investing_ in myself and my future—by creating that _energetic exchange_—I made myself available for more money, and high-vibe clients, to find me. As a result, five-figure months are now a consistent part of my income structure.

I owe a lot of this to taking the time to reframe how I've thought about money. Our thoughts are so incredibly powerful, so we must make sure we're feeding ourselves positive, abundant, anything-is-possible type thoughts. You shouldn't settle for anything less, and if you are, it's time you participated in my three Rs: review, reframe, and renew.

REVIEW: Take some time to review your money stories. What did your parents tell you with regards to money when you were growing up? That it's important to save, rather than spend? That you should never spend more than you earn? That you can't make a living doing what you love? Write 'em all down.

REFRAME: Let's say you were told growing up that **money can't buy happiness**. In order to reframe this thought, we need to question our belief in it. So, what is it that makes you happy? For me, I'm happiest when I'm traveling the world, experiencing new cultures, visiting family and friends, writing and publishing my books, and helping others to achieve their dreams. Does money help me to achieve any of these things? Yes, absolutely. Money helps me buy plane tickets to travel, experience new cultures, and visit family and friends. Money helps me to afford a laptop, an editor, a cover designer, and much more for my books. Money also helps me to create great teaching programs using best-in-class website platforms and CRM systems. So, this thought should be reframed as: **Money *supports* my happiness** because it helps me do the things that make me happy.

RENEW: Once you've reframed the limiting beliefs around your money stories, it can be easy to relapse if you don't make them a daily part of your life. Journal your reframed money mantras daily. Say them out loud in the mirror or on your drive to work. Write them in your planner, or make them the background on your phone. It takes *time* to replace one agreement (your limiting money story) with a new one (your reframed money story). Just like the roots of a tree, that original agreement/belief is grounded into your core being. But with time, persistence, patience, and "reframing" that old belief, new roots will begin to form and branch out.

BYOG ACTION 50: Write down your "whys" for wanting more money. How do these "whys" affect your life? Do they affect other people as well? Is the overall effect positive or negative?

BYOG ACTION 51: You've probably found that the overall effect of your "whys" is positive. If you start to feel gross/greedy/selfish for wanting more money, refer back to this list. Remind yourself of all the *good* that will come from you receiving more money.

BYOG ACTION 52: Forgive negative experiences around money. Forgive your parents, teachers, grandparents, whoever fed you *their* negative money stories. The next time someone tries to relay their money experiences to you or make you believe them, take a step back. Realize that this is *their* money story, not yours.

Remind yourself that they can play small all they want, but you're here to play BIG.

Closing Thought :

Money is simply energy.
So let it flow, easily and
effortlessly, into your life.

chapter fourteen

SET YOUR SOUL ABLAZE

LETTING YOURSELF RUN rampant and free sounds amazing, doesn't it? Imagine if you weren't tied down by responsibilities, the pains of adulting, bills, jobs . . . anything would be possible. You could do whatever your heart desired—

Tap the brakes!

What if I told you that you *can* do whatever your heart desires *right now*—at this very moment—and that the only thing holding you back . . . is you?

I see so many people wait for the "perfect" time—more money, more freedom, what they envision to be a better version of themselves. This "perfect" scenario that you've dreamed up in your head—the one where you have stacks on stacks of cash in your reserves, where your kids are grown and living on their own, where you have more *freedom* to pursue your passions . . .

This "perfect time" you've conjured up in your head?

It doesn't exist.

That situation is imaginary—it is not real. What *is* real is the life you're living this very instant; and if there's something you don't like about it, it's time to buck up and make some much-needed changes.

Setting your soul ablaze means understanding that the current circumstances of your situation do not define who you are as a person, nor do they define where you're headed. If anything, it's the opposite—you, as a person, and wherever it is you want to go in life, are responsible for your circumstances. What we focus on, we create more of. Once again, like attracts like. Meaning if you're stuck in a shitty situation, I hate to break it to you, but **you're the one who put yourself there.**

We can redefine our situations and our circumstances at any moment—but I'll warn you, it's not going to be a walk in the park. The easy thing to do would be to wallow in self-pity about how much your life sucks, your relationship/marriage sucks, your job sucks, and so on. That's taking the easy way out. The hard thing to do is put on your big-girl pants, figure your shit out, and get your life together.

I may come off as a little harsh in the writing of this chapter, but it's because this topic is one that, yet again, really fires me up. Remember reading in an earlier chapter about living a mediocre existence, where I was throwing F-bombs left and right? Setting your soul ablaze falls right into that category, so get ready to dodge these flaming F-missiles!

Setting your soul ablaze means going on a spiritual journey—discovering who you truly are, what your core desires are, and how far you're willing to go to get them. It means pushing through the fear of rejection, judgment, and that feeling of not being "enough", and doing the damn thing anyway. It means pursuing what lights you up from within, what makes your heart happy, and making time for it **every single day**, no matter the cost. It means you're willing to make mistakes, and potentially be humiliated, because that's the only way you'll learn, grow, and elevate to the next level. It means being absolutely fearless in the pursuit of what sets your soul on fire.

As I've alluded to throughout this book, I flailed throughout each and every phase in my life, like a tiny little bird readying itself to leave the nest and drop off into its first flight. I did certain things because other people *told* me I should be doing them. I behaved a certain way because society told me that was how I was supposed to be. I lost myself, over and over again, until eventually, I'd been lost so many times that the hope of being found withered away. I created and recreated myself, all to fit a certain "mold"—to make sure I was honoring the *agreements* that'd I'd subconsciously said yes to throughout my childhood, even though they weren't my own. I ignored red flags in relationships and friendships because I wanted to be a kind and good person—because everyone deserves second chances, right?

Wrong.

Not everyone does, especially those who treat you like dirt. I stayed in toxic situations because "maybe I can fix them". If you actually sit and write down *all* of the things you've unknowingly agreed to—these things that have become your steadfast *truths*—you'll quickly realize that they've been running your life since you entered this world wailing and screaming. It'll be enough to make you want to crawl back into the womb and stay there.

Setting your soul ablaze means you have to get **real**, and—as much as I dislike this word—*intimate* with yourself. You'll have to learn how to block out external distractions and chatter, and how to discern when someone is trying to imprint *their* perception of reality and "the way the world works" on you—because this is something that happens almost every waking moment of our lives.

From the text conversation you have with your best friend in the morning, to the lunch meeting with your boss, to the social media posts of friends, family, and complete strangers—someone else's perception of reality is *always* in front of you, trying to wiggle its way into your mind and imprint itself as a part of *your* reality.

Your perception of reality is **sacred**. If it feels right in your heart, and you know it to be true, don't allow externalities to skew it. Protect it. Cherish it.

Because it is yours, and yours alone.

It's taken me two full years of really hunkering down on my spiritual journey for me to get to a place where I am truly comfortable in my own skin. I am confident in my thoughts and the words I speak and the actions I take. I am no longer easily persuaded or manipulated by the white noise of society and its judgments and expectations. Setting your soul ablaze is about *living for yourself* and no one else.

Unfortunately, there's no roadmap for this. I've said it before and I'll say it again—we're all just making it up as we go. Your parents, your grandparents, that influencer on social media you look up to—all had zero clue about what they were doing when they were doing it. Raising you and your brothers and sisters? Zero clue. Starting a business? Zero clue. Deciding which way to go after reaching a fork in the road? Zero clue.

But the *one thing* they all have in common? Listening to their hearts. Fighting their egos and their fear-based stories. Leaping into the unknown. That's what you do when you have kids, right? I don't have kids myself, but I can imagine that even after reading *all* of the parenting books in the world, you'd probably end up throwing the advice to the wind the first week in. Why? Because every situation is *different* and requires us to tap into our intuition—that inner guiding voice—to make choices that feel best at that specific time.

But that's the beauty of it! Whatever it is you want to set out to do, I can guarantee hasn't been done before in the *exact* way that you're going to do it. The way you execute your path will be completely different from your sister's or your friend's. And that's a beautiful thing.

My journey to get where I am today is unique to me— it is my path and no one else's. I didn't want a blueprint because that would have been *boring*. Seriously, gouge my eyes out with a fork right now. I wouldn't have learned half the things I now know to be true about myself, my business, and my life in general—and those things were all necessary for me to learn in order to truly *understand* what I want for my life and how I'm going to make it a reality.

Blueprints are for building houses—when you're looking for an exact outline to take X and Y materials to get outcome Z. Trailblazing is for your *life*—it's messy, chaotic, and you're whacking down tree branches with a machete. Hell, a lot of the time you have no idea if the decision you just made is the right one, but it was *your* decision to make, *your* mistake to potentially be made, and *your* lesson to learn. We can seek guidance along the way—and in fact, I encourage it—but do not allow having an "exact" strategy to throw a wrench in your plans for starting. The most memorable parts of my journey are actually the mistakes I've made—and, while I felt like a fool at the time, those mistakes were necessary for me to learn so that I could grow and elevate my life and business.

If you're having trouble "setting your soul ablaze" for the first time, I want you to ask yourself one question that may seem simple on the outside, but when you think about it, is actually quite loaded. And that question is:

> ### If you had all the money in the world, and you knew that this influx of money would continue to arrive in your bank account each and every month, <u>what would you be doing with your life</u>?

This question, in a nutshell, is asking you to *remove* the money struggle and your focus on "lack of money" and shift it to a place of abundance, of *knowing* that the universe will support you—that all of your financial and material needs will be met as required. This question is asking you—with the thought of money completely removed—what your passions are. What would you be doing with your life? What makes you happy at your core? When do you feel the most *in flow*? And again, how often are you doing those things that really light you up?

As we discussed in the previous chapter, money is a

huge force in our existence and, sadly, it runs how a lot of people live their lives. We get so focused on *saving* our money and ensuring that we'll have "enough" for the future that we forget to enjoy it and spend it on the *now*— right *now*, this *present moment*, is all we're guaranteed.

I'll say that again.

This present moment is all we're guaranteed.

Tomorrow is a relative term. Tomorrow doesn't exist. It is not promised nor is it guaranteed. And while I understand the desire to build a nest egg for the future, **do not let saving keep you from living**. Investing in yourself and your passions, both from a financial aspect and a time aspect, is the *best thing* you can do for yourself.

And you can do it **right now**.

If you feel that there are obstacles standing directly in your way, or hurdles that you have to jump over, write down what they are. Go back to chapter one and review those BYOG actions. The more you familiarize yourself with what's stopping you and what your hesitations are, the more you'll recognize when they crop up and try to derail you.

The last thing I want to touch on when it comes to setting your soul ablaze is: innovation. And I know this can sound like a scary word, but bear with me. As a trailblazer of your own life and passions, an innovative mindset is not only desirable—it is *crucial*. Every morning when you wake up, you'll need to come up with new ideas and different ways of doing things. You'll need to become the master of your schedule and the protector of your time. You'll need to try and fail, then try and fail again. Repeat twenty-two times until something sticks and then—LEVEL UP!

You can now pass GO. You can now collect $200.

Blazing your own trail also means keeping an open mind. It means seeking out resources, tools, and knowledge to help guide you in the right direction. You'll need to be innovative to find these resources, tools, and knowledge, but with the internet at our fingertips, it's all in a day's (or hour's) work.

Innovation is key in the way that you engage with your audience, persuade people to trust and ultimately buy from you, and execute new strategies and push for new directions to reach that next level of growth. Comparison can, and *will*, get in the way, and when (not if) it does, make sure to review chapter eleven and those BYOG actions to remember what you stand for and why you're here.

Write down your WHY. Create a mission statement. Develop a business plan. Try and fail, dust yourself off, then get back up and try again. Maintain that innovative spirit and that open mind, and you will go further than you ever thought possible.

BYOG ACTION 53: What perceptions of reality (from others) have you been holding onto? What truths have you subconsciously agreed to since childhood? If they serve you, write down why. If they don't, reframe them into new truths.

BYOG ACTION 54: Write down every single thing that makes you happy, no matter how trivial. It may be listening to thunder on rainy days, drinking tea by the fireplace, snuggling up with your furbabies and kids at night, or getting engrossed in a really good book. It may also be traveling the world, shopping, or buying gifts for loved ones. But most likely, the majority of what makes you happy won't actually *cost any money*, so vow to yourself to incorporate those things into your day-to-day. When you start to base your happiness on *experiences* instead of things, an entirely new way of living will present itself to you.

BYOG ACTION 55: How can you be more *innovative* in your day-to-day? What knowledge can you glean? What resources can you utilize? Make a promise to yourself to try new things, especially when you feel stuck, whether it's in your life, relationship, work, passion, or business. Keep a running list of *new* things to try for each category and when you feel yourself falling into the abyss of zero motivation, refer to your list and change things up a bit.

BYOG ACTION 56: Be fearless. Write down all the things *Fearless You* would do if you weren't worried about failure, judgment, debt, lack of time, etc. Whenever you're feeling afraid, refer back to this list and remember that we can't take anything with us—no material item, no debt, no problems—so what do you really have to lose?

Closing Thought :

Be fearless in the pursuit of
what sets your soul on fire.

chapter fifteen

SHOW UP EVERY DAY

IT GOES WITHOUT saying that setting your soul ablaze is pointless if you're not going to show up every day! You may be thinking, "Of course I'm going to show up, Kristen. I wake up, get ready, and get on with my day."

No, no, no. This isn't even *close* to what I'm talking about.

It is entirely possible (and I've seen it happen more times than I'd like) to set your soul ablaze for a week, maybe a month, and then fall off the wagon when things get rough or don't go your way. I've seen this happen with family members, with friends, with significant others—where they'd gotten an idea and were so psyched about it, they'd pursued it at warped speed for about a week, and then the *second* a roadblock presented itself, they'd said, "Well, I guess this is a sign that this is not what I'm supposed to be doing. Back to the drawing board."

WHAT?!

Oh, the times I wanted to violently shake people and slap 'em across the side of the head are too many for me to count. There is a *massive* difference in a **red flag** and a **purposeful obstacle.**

A **red flag** is your intuition, your gut, that inner voice, telling you that something IS indeed very wrong and that you need to get the hell outta dodge. This could be, say, your significant other making the same mistake over and over again, one that *really* could impact both of your lives if they continue down that path and don't stop. It could also be an opportunity or offer that just doesn't *feel* right—it's shady, underhanded, and obtuse. A red flag is loud and glaringly obvious. It's your heart and your head screaming at you to:

STOP THE TRAIN. GET OFF THE TRAIN. BOARD A PLANE INSTEAD!

A **purposeful obstacle**, however, is a roadblock that pops up because *there is something you need to learn* before leveling up, before moving onto the *next phase* of your life, your relationship, or whatever the situation may be. It tends to be very direct, but a little quieter. It's a rejection (usually when someone tells you no), or a judgment (when someone tells you that you aren't good enough), or a perceived failure (when something doesn't work out like you'd expected). It's a whisper that says, "Okay, so that didn't go as planned, but that's because it wasn't the right time/opportunity/event for you in your current situation, *but* it's something to work toward. What steps can you take to work toward that?"

A great example of a red flag in my own life is my most recent failed relationship. All the signs of alcoholism were there, and I remember my heart and mind screaming at me to GET OUT NOW, but I shoved the screaming down so far that I ultimately silenced it. Every time I spoke with my parents on the phone about my relationship, I could feel that turmoil in my stomach, and I knew deep down that something wasn't right—but I'd continue to put on a happy face, even though shit was hitting the fan left and right.

I pushed my perceptions of reality onto him, and tried to make him see that there was a different and better way—a different life path than the one he'd been living. I desperately clung to my sense of control, trying to change this person I was supposed to be in love with and **make** him see what I saw he could be. **But you cannot change a person.**

People only change if *they*, deep down, **want to change**. It's up to them. Not you. Ignoring that inner turmoil allowed it to fester, and I got so far down the path with this person (engagement) that it ultimately blew up in my face, into a wedding, and a future, that never happened.

Red flag, red flag, red flag.

An example of a purposeful obstacle in my life would be getting rejected by literary agents over and over again. I'd always thought that in order to become an author, one **had to be** traditionally published. I hadn't even realized that another path (indie/self-publishing) existed. Instead of quitting my dream of becoming an author altogether, I said, "There has to be another way and I'm going to find it."

Flash forward to now where I'm a bestselling self-published author, my own boss, and happier than I've ever been.

Do we see the difference?

Red flag versus purposeful obstacle.

Now, learning how to *distinguish* between the two takes a lot of time, patience, and experience. It takes *learning* how to listen to that inner voice and *processing* the feelings that come up. I stayed in a toxic relationship for far too long because I was too damn stubborn to succumb to the power of the red flags. I wanted something (a partner and a future) so badly that I was willing to forego the *right partner and future* for a relationship that wasn't serving me in the first place. But, from that experience, I now know what a red flag *for me* actually feels like. I can sense it and detect it from a mile away. I've talked about that roiling in my stomach and tightness in my chest—so for me, red flags show up in the physical sense. They also show up in my mind, when I have that flicker of doubt or brief moment of dread about a certain person or situation. Don't ignore those feelings. They are signs—signs you need to learn to listen to so you can avoid getting involved in something that *will* eventually cause major destruction in your life.

At some point in our lives, I think we all end up rushing toward a red flag when really we should turn the other direction and walk away from it—and that experience will likely be the most heart-wrenching, but also the most necessary, because it's only reason for showing up is to ensure that you are 100% clear on what a red flag *feels* like **for you**. How can we know if we've never felt it?

Hindsight is 20/20.

I digress. That was a bit of a tangent, but the point of me bringing this up is because I've witnessed so many people stop pursuing their passions because of what they *thought* was a red flag, when really it was just a **purposeful obstacle**. It was almost as if they were too afraid to peek over the wall, to learn what was on the other side—and if they'd just done that in the first place, they'd be leagues beyond their wildest dreams in their lives, passions, careers, and businesses.

When you can take roadblocks for what they actually are (purposeful obstacles), it makes it so much easier to show up for yourself and your passions every single day. When you decide you're going to do something, you have to go as far in as you possibly can. Notice how I didn't say "all in" because I feel like there's a huge misconception out there about "going all in" when it comes to your passion. For example, I would have been certifiably insane to "go all in" when I published my debut novel in 2015.

Well guys, I did it. I'm publishing my book. I'm quitting my job and going all in because I'll have this one book published and it will be enough to pay the bills and continue living the lifestyle I've become accustomed to living.

One ticket to **crazy-town**, please and thank you.

It's great to have a passion. It's great to have a dream and a vision for your life. But *good things take time*. There needs to be a realistic aspect to your dreams, otherwise you'll end up throwing yourself overboard before the ship has even set sail.

What I mean by going "as far in as you possibly can" is *making as much time possible* to work toward your passion and your dreams. It means saying no to things you *really* want to say yes to. It means waking up an hour earlier before work. It means staying up two hours later once the kids have been put to bed. It means using your weekends wisely and not binge-watching a million seasons of The Bachelor.

By the same token, it shouldn't be difficult to *make time* for your passions and your dreams *if* they're something that you **really want for yourself.** It should be a no-brainer. On any given day, I would rather write, create content, and work on my author platform than do *anything else*. Yes, that includes hanging out with people, going to brunch, watching TV, and shopping. I actually go weeks without stepping foot into the mall (or shopping on Amazon) and I go days without turning on the TV. I read and write instead. Just like we discussed in chapter five, time is your friend—it's all about how you decide to use it.

So what does it look like when you show up for yourself every day? It's going to look different for everyone, but for me, showing up looks like:

Exercising first thing when I wake up

Making my bed

Meditating and journaling

Setting my intentions for the day

Showering, styling my hair, and getting ready

Cooking a healthy breakfast

Writing/creating content for at least 2-3 hours
Taking a break to read or call a friend/family
Spending time outdoors (walking Denali)
Trying at least one new thing a week
Booking travel/vacations at least 3 times a year

When you can nail down your ideal day/routine, and act on it, showing up for yourself becomes habitual. Of course, there are some days where something unexpected will pop up and may take a decent chunk of time out of your schedule, but as long as you don't wallow in the pit of un-productivity and get back to kicking ass, doing the things you love, you can't **not** show up for yourself.

I should mention, though, that showing up every day does require one teensy little thing that will take some practice—your mindset. I'm sure you've had those days where you *just don't feel like it*. You just don't feel like getting ready, or going to the gym, or writing, or answering emails (which, by the way, does anyone actually *like* answering emails?)—but just as manifestation requires activation, so does showing up.

You have to **make the decision** to show up every day.

There's a switch in your brain that only you can flip on to say, "Okay, let's do this, even though I don't feel like it." This ability to shift from a place of *not doing* to *doing* is where the true secret of successful people lies. As Stephen King says, "Amateurs sit and wait for inspiration, the rest of us just get up and go to work."

If you find yourself always waiting for inspiration and motivation, **you will never get anywhere.** You will start and stop something more times than you can count. And you'll feel frustrated each time because you can't possibly understand **why** you're not making progress. You'll find all the flaws in the world related to what you're doing and why it isn't working, when the only reason it's not working is because **you're not showing up fully.**

Showing up every day is a conscious decision. It's not something that just happens. *But,* if you make the decision often enough, it will become a habit, and a welcome one at that.

As I've practiced this, now when I wake up in the mornings, I don't even think about what I'm going to do that day. I do exactly what I shared in my ideal routine (except for Sundays because those are my self-care days). It's habit for me. It's automatic. And if you're wondering how I arrived at this stage, I'm going to share something I learned a while ago that's made all the difference.

The 5 Second Rule by Mel Robbins.

Let me guess you're thinking—*is she talking about how it's okay to eat food that you've dropped on the floor, as long as it's only been on the floor for 5 seconds or less?* Nope, we're not talking about *that* 5-second rule.

The basis of The 5 Second Rule is that the moment we have an instinct to act on a goal, we must physically move within five seconds or your brain will stop you. And how does Mel propose we do this? By counting backwards from five.

5-4-3-2-1. I'm going to write 1,000 words today.

5-4-3-2-1. I'm going to run 1 mile this morning.

5-4-3-2-1. I'm going to finish this essay today.

It sounds crazy, but it actually works, and it's something I've been doing over the past couple of years.

Now, in order for it to work, the instinct must be tied to a goal. So, in the examples above, you do these things because your larger goals are likely finishing or publishing a book, losing weight or getting in shape, or getting good grades in school so you can get into the college of your choice.

The reason counting down works is because it will focus your mind on the goal or commitment and, albeit momentarily, it distracts you from the worries, doubts, thoughts, and excuses circulating in your mind. That 5-second window is just enough time to get you focused on your goal and *wanting* to act on it as opposed to talking yourself out of why you shouldn't or don't want to do it at that moment in time.

The next time you're struggling to work on something that contributes to a larger goal of yours, try The 5 Second Rule. Take a deep breath and count down from five, set your intention (say it out loud if you need to), then stand up and go do whatever it is you've been putting off. This rule changed the game when it comes to my productivity, and I believe it can do the same for you.

Let's say you revisit this chapter after you've been showing up consistently for quite some time for your passions and your dreams. As you show up and elevate your life and business, certain things in your routine may need to change. Why?

Because every next level of your life will demand a different you.

So my current day-to-day routine *right now* may look very different in the next couple of years, especially if I'm traveling to more speaking engagements, or hosting workshops, or going on international book tours to meet my readers in person. I may need more self-care days. I may need to hire a team of people—an assistant, a publicist—to help me in managing my author platform. As your life and your status elevates, so will you. You can't have one without the other—one doesn't even *exist* without the other.

If, for any reason, you start to feel stagnant, like you're not moving forward, it may be time to reassess how you're spending your days. Are minutiae bogging down your day to the point where you can't take part in value-adding activities? Are you stretched for time? Are you pulling all-nighters, coming way too close to deadlines?

If so, it may be because you've been channeling your inner Superwoman for so long that you've become blind to the fact that, due to your tremendous growth in your life/passion/business, you now need to outsource some things.

Only *you* will be able to determine what the "next level you" looks like, and if you get it wrong the first time around, it's okay. Tweak, make adjustments, and keep making changes until it feels right.

How will you know when it's right? Simple. You'll feel fulfilled, happy, and balanced.

But in order to get there . . . you've gotta show up.

BYOG ACTION 57: Given your current situation, what does your ideal routine look like *right now*? Write down all the things you would like to accomplish in a day, plus all the things you currently *have* to do (like your job, dropping the kids off at school, etc.)

BYOG ACTION 58: This may take some brainpower, but try to plan ahead. What would your ideal day look like a year from now? Three years from now? For instance, if you're currently in a job that you're desperate to get out of, but currently need the cash to pay the bills, your routine probably consists of working for eight hours. Maybe six months down the road, you can negotiate a longer lunch break so you'll have some free time to work on your passion (which would be a change in your ideal routine). In a year, perhaps your ideal routine would be having the freedom to work remotely. In three years, perhaps your ideal routine will have nothing to do with your current job because you've quit and have elevated to the next level of your life and business. When you take the time to lay your vision out in front of you, you can more clearly see what it is you're working towards—and it makes it easier to figure out how you can get there.

BYOG ACTION 59: Make a list of the things that you do to self-sabotage your productivity or your progress. These could be things like watching TV or mindlessly scrolling through social media when *really* you should be writing, drawing, creating, or working on your passion. Or it could be thought patterns, like doubting yourself, judging your work, or convincing yourself that you're too tired, unmotivated, or lazy. When you become aware of your self-sabotaging habits, you can catch them in their midst and implement The 5 Second Rule.

BYOG ACTION 60: If all else fails, **take action**. Even if it's something small, **take action**. More often than not, that action will create a snowball effect and you'll continue working on things, moving onto the next project, that next task on your to-do list, ultimately driving you closer to your goals and where you want to be.

Closing Thought :

"Showing up fully, exactly
where you are, is the fastest way
to get you where you want to go."

–Marie Forleo

closing thoughts

FROM THE AUTHOR

YOU DID IT. You made it to the end of this book. How do you feel? Inspired? Motivated? Frustrated that you've waited until now to realize that everything you've ever needed to live your dream life has been inside of you all along?

These are all perfectly understandable reactions, but more than anything, I hope you feel *empowered* and ready to kick some ass and do the damn thing—whatever that *thing* is, only you know!

So, if we had to sum it up, what does **Be Your Own #Goals** really boil down to? If there's one thing I want you to take away from this book, it's this:

YOU ARE ENOUGH.

The person you were in the past was enough then, and the person you are present day is enough right now. The person you'll become in three, ten, twenty years down the road is *enough*. You don't need anyone's permission or approval to live the way *you* want to live. Don't waste this one precious life comparing your life to the highlight reel of others. Stay in your own lane. Do you, and only strive to be better than the person you were yesterday. You don't need to wait for the right time, financial situation, or experience level because it DOES NOT EXIST. You are enough, this moment right now is enough, and you need to grab the bull by the horns because honey, we ain't gettin' any younger!

Remember that the future is *never* guaranteed, and that all we know *for sure* is what's before us in this very moment. So why wait? Why prolong it any further?

If you're unhappy, make a change. Choices and opportunities are all around you, and present themselves more often than you might think—we just don't always notice them. Some will flash brightly in neon lights, and others will be a faint whisper that may require sharpening your listening skills to hear. Take the time to uncover those faint whispers. Pay attention. Keep your ear to the ground and your heart in the sky.

Remember that you get one chance at this. Just ONE. So your life should be nothing less than miraculous and awe-inspiring. If you're not jumping out of bed in the morning to start your day and hitting the ground running, it's time to reassess. It's time to journey deep within your psyche, to the depths of your heart, and discover what *truly* lights you up—not what other people *say* lights you up, but what truly, unequivocally makes you COME ALIVE. Be fearless in the pursuit of what sets your soul on fire—and NEVER apologize for it. EVER.

I said it once, and I'll say it again. Screw the judgments. Screw the negativity. Screw the drama. Screw the FEAR. If there's something you want to do, whether it's write a book, build your dream business, or get that seemingly impossibly promotion—GO FOR IT. Do not waste another breath second-guessing yourself and your worth. The world needs your talent, your leadership, your voice—and by playing small and playing it "safe", you're only robbing the world of a message they so desperately need to hear; a product that will change their lives for the better; a service that will inspire more creation to benefit generations to come. Go for it and hold nothing back.

Drop your issues surrounding money. Money is not good or bad—it just *is*. It's a *resource* that allows us to enrich the lives of others, as well as our own, because it provides access to opportunities that most people could only dream of. The sooner you realize and rewrite your current money stories, the sooner (and easier) money will flow to you. Abundance is your natural birthright. You are worthy of all your financial and material desires. Money doesn't have to be a struggle, and the only one keeping it on the struggle-train is YOU.

Likewise, if something is no longer serving you, like a relationship, a friendship, or a job—love yourself enough to cut ties. Have the courage to walk away. There's ZERO room for toxic energy when you're building your empire, so let that shit go, and FAST. Trust me when I say that it's easier to do it *now*, than to wait another year when you feel more "ready". You'll never feel fully ready to hurt someone you care about. But if they're draining you, keeping them in your life is only hurting *you*—which is in direct conflict with the overarching theme of this book in that . . .

YOU COME FIRST.
ALWAYS.

Don't forget to take care of yourself, especially on the days where you need it most. Take yourself on a date. Buy yourself a fresh bouquet of roses. Treat yourself to a spa day. When you're operating at your highest frequency and as your best self, everyone around you will cultivate a similar energy and, like a magnet, they'll stick to you.

So this, my dear friends, is what I want to leave you with.

Be **PROUD** of who you are.

Be **INSPIRED** by where you came from.

Be **DRIVEN** by how far you're going to go.

Be **RELENTLESS** in pursuing your best life.

And lastly, but most importantly . . .

Be **FEARLESS** in becoming your own #GOALS.

acknowledgements

As someone who started off writing fiction, it's no surprise that this book required me to unlock a very different part of myself as a writer. While being so raw and vulnerable was terrifying at times, it feels 100% worth it knowing that it might help even *one* person out there who may relate to some of the struggles I've had.

First and foremost, I'd like to thank God, The Universe, The Divine—my spiritual journey over the past four years has been nothing short of miraculous, and the guidance I've received has been astounding. Blessed is a severe understatement.

To Kaila Walker, for being an amazing mentor, for writing the foreword, and for being such an advocate of this book. I cannot thank you enough for inspiring me to finally finish this project. I am forever grateful for our friendship and how close we've become in such a short amount of time. You inspire me to be better and live better every day! Parsnip Whippers fo' lyfe!

To Anna Vera, for our meet-ups in Arizona and our 5-hour Skype dates over wine, I cannot even tell you how awe-struck I am that we walked into each others' lives. I feel like I can tell you *anything* and *everything*, which is rare in and of itself. You are my Taurean soul sister, and you inspire me to be a better writer every day!

To Kim Chance, for being there during my hard days and for listening wholeheartedly when I need to rant! You've created such a safe space for me to express myself (and my many feelings) and I am so blessed to call you one of my closest friends! Love you, girl!

To Vivien Reis, my beta reader turned soulsister! I'd always hoped we would meet in person one day because I just knew we'd instantly click. I can't wait to continue collaborating and working on projects together—the future is so bright, my dear!

To my AuthorTube family—Lindsay Cummings, Jessi Elliott, Natalia Leigh, Mandi Lynn, and so many more—I feel so blessed to be a part of such an amazing community, and that we can fully lean on each other when needed. A close-knit community was definitely something I was missing in the earlier part of my author career. You guys are my #SOULTRIBE, and I feel so fortunate to call each and every one of you my friend.

To my family—Erin, Mom, Paul, Dad, Rachel, Nana and Papa—thank you for being such an incredible support system. I know I'm definitely a dreamer and that I don't always see the "realistic" side of things, but I like that I can fly to AZ or CA whenever I need to get grounded again. I love you and appreciate you more than you will ever know.

To my Valiance members—thank you for believing in me and my coaching program. I've enjoyed working with each of you immensely, and I cannot wait to see the amazing books you write and put out into the world!

To my Podcast supporters—thank you for being so kind and open to the ramblings of my crazy little brain. You've cultivated such a safe space for me that I feel like I can share anything—and you're a large part of the reason as to why I decided to finish writing this book in the first place, so THANK YOU!

To my YouTube fam—thank you for sticking by me and for continuing to watch my videos and engage in conversation on my channel! The fullness and love I feel every time I post a new video is indescribable, and it's all thanks to you!

And lastly, to my readers—your enthusiasm for my books, whether fiction or nonfiction, inspires me to keep going, to keep creating. Your support fuels my creativity, and there is not a single day I wake up and take this life for granted. I cannot express my gratitude enough. Thank you for allowing me to share my message. Thank you for sharing my books with your friends and family. And thank you for allowing, accepting, and encouraging me to be unapologetically the truest version of myself.

That Smart Hustle

For more *girlboss vibes* and tips on *designing your dream life*, make sure to check out *Kristen's podcast*, That Smart Hustle!

Available to listen on iTunes and SoundCloud

Hustle Smarter, Not Harder

Are you ready to …

Discover your *passion*?

Find tangible ways to turn that passion into *profit*?

Manage your time like a *boss*?

Actually *LIVE* the life you've always *dreamed*?

Sign up for Kristen's

Hustle Smarter, Not Harder Webinar Series

at http://www.thatsmarthustle.com

Valiance Coaching Program

Done pulling your hair out trying to write your book?
You're not alone! Kristen's extensive self-study
coaching program for writers, Valiance, is the
blueprint you've been searching for to finally
write & publish the book of your heart.

To learn more and sign up, go to:

http://www.kristenmartinbooks/valiance-coaching-program

about the author

Kristen Martin is the international Amazon bestselling author of the young adult science fiction trilogy, THE ALPHA DRIVE, the dark fantasy series, SHADOW CROWN, and the self-help book, BE YOUR OWN #GOALS. She is also a writing coach (Valiance), the founder of That Smart Hustle, and an avid YouTuber with hundreds of videos offering inspirational writing advice for aspiring authors.

STAY CONNECTED:

www.kristenmartinbooks.com
www.youtube.com/authorkristenmartinbooks
www.facebook.com/authorkristenmartin
Instagram @authorkristenmartin
Twitter @authorkristenm